Information
and the Muslim World

A Strategy for the Twenty-first Century

Ziauddin Sardar

Mansell Publishing Limited
London and New York

First published 1988 by Mansell Publishing Limited
6 All Saints Street, London N1 9RL, England
950 University Avenue, Bronx, New York 10452, U.S.A.

British Library Cataloguing in Publication Data

Sardar, Ziauddin
  Information and the Muslim world : a strategy for the twenty-first century.
  1. Information services—Islamic countries
  I. Title
  025.5′2′0917671   Z674.5.I8

  ISBN 0-7201-1728-3

Library of Congress Cataloging in Publication Data

Sardar, Ziauddin.
  Information and the Muslim world.

  Bibliography: p.
  Includes index.
  1. Information services—Islamic countries—Planning. 2. Information
services and state—Islamic countries. 3. Libraries and state—Islamic
countries. 4. Communication policy—Islamic countries. 5. Library
planning—Islamic countries. 6. Islamic countries—Information services—
Planning. I. Title.
Z674.5.I74S27 1987   020′.917′671   87–28295
ISBN 0-7201-1728-3

This book has been printed and bound in Great Britain:
Typeset in Plantin by Colset Private Limited, printed on Windrush Antique
Book Wove Cream paper by Biddles Ltd., Guildford

Islamic Futures and Policy Studies

Series editor, *Ziauddin Sardar*

Director, Center for Policy and Future Studies
East-West University, Chicago

By the same author

Science, Technology and Development in the Muslim World
Hajj Studies, editor
Muhammad: Aspects of a Biography
Islam: Outline of a Classification Scheme
Science and Technology in the Middle East
The Future of Muslim Civilization
The Touch of Midas, editor
Islamic Futures: the Shape of Ideas to Come

For Janet Rennie, Penelope Yates-Mercer and R. T. Bottle,
who taught me most of the information science I know

Contents

List of Figures and Tables

Preface

Information and the Muslim World has its origins in the keynote address
to the second Congress of Muslim Librarians and Information Scientists (COMLIS II, Universiti Utara Malaysia, Alos Ator, 20–22 October
1986). The Congress, which had gathered together most of the pro-
minent Muslim librarians and information scientists, concluded that
a coherent and well thought-out information strategy was needed for the
Muslim world if information science is to become relevant to the needs
and requirements of Muslim societies. A strategy is needed not just to
avoid duplication among Muslim states, conserve valuable resources
and promote co-operation, but, as information is rapidly becoming the
basic commodity of our time, for the very survival of the Muslim world
as an independent entity, indeed a civilization. Moreover, to convince all
sectors of society, the traditional leadership as well as modern decision-
makers, of the importance of the generation and free flow of information
in the contemporary world, the role of information in Muslim societies
must be analysed from the perspective of Islam and some of its important
universal concepts. I hope that the strategy outlined in this book and
the analysis offered meet the requirements and the standards set at
COMLIS II.

As this is a book on the role of information in development, and not on
development *per se*, I have not discussed in detail the failure of many
conventional development strategies, such as the transfer of technology
and the contribution of the Green Revolution, but simply referred the

reader to sources which provide adequate analysis. (I analysed the short-comings of conventional development schemes a decade ago in *Science Technology and Development in the Muslim World*.) Instead, I have evolved my own basic needs orientated model of development, based on the essential concepts of Islam, and used this model as a tool for under-standing the role of information in Muslim societies. Much of the development in the Muslim world, over the last three decades, has been at the expense of basic needs and the rural population. I believe that it is not possible to go forward to the twenty-first century without redressing this balance.

I would like to give special thanks to my friends Anwar Ibrahim, Minister of Education in Malaysia, for encouraging me and supporting the work of COMLIS II — indeed, for being the first decision-maker to implement some of its recommendations; and Oli Mohammad, President of COMLIS, for insisting that I write this book. Thanks are also due to my colleague and dear friend, Munawar Ahmad Anees, who was always there when I needed him.

Introduction
Challenging a Cliché

It has now become a cliché to say that we are living in an information age. The invention of the microchip and the consequent development of the microcomputer has unleashed an awesome power that enables access to information at the touch of a button. There is a wide consensus that new computer technologies will inevitably reshape our future, lead us to redefine work and leisure, and in the long run, thought and knowledge as well. This future will be created by the fusion of two hitherto separate fields which are now merging: computer science and telecommunications. The advent of the microcomputer revolutionized computer science by dramatically altering the cost/performance and volume/performance ratio. The smaller the chip, the cheaper it is and the more power it has. When smaller and smaller microcomputers are combined with innovations in telecommunications — satellites, telephony, cable, fibre optics, etc. — a rapidly advancing 'electronic highway' is created, allowing multiple long-distance usage and greatly decentralized production patterns. All this makes the generation, transfer, manipulation, control of and access to information, literally, child's play.

The 'information revolution' is being sold as highly advantageous for mankind. The hard sell on television, in newspapers and glossy magazines is inviting. Consider the advertisement for a micro- and mini-computer in a Paris newspaper which praised its products for 'softness' and went on: 'a supple infotech, like a reed which will bend in response to sudden strains; a crystal-clear infotech which guarantees transparent management; a chameleon infotech which will react quickly to changes; a finely tuned infotech like a violin which respects human sensibility . . .' It is not a computer that one is buying but a life–long companion which can solve all one's problems and all one's needs. This type of message is given intellectual respectability by such books as Alvin Toffler's *The Third Wave* and Jean-Jacques Servan-Schreiber's *Le Défi Mondial*. In learned circles, research journals and academic books it is argued that the information revolution will lead to decentralization and hence to a more democratic society, increased cultural diversity by providing access to a whole range of information to suit all needs, and give people an opportunity to develop new skills, increase production and thus generate wealth for the benefit of all. It will transform society radically into becoming more humane and enlightened. The proliferation of new information technology will lead to a new electronic civilization, a quantum leap to a higher level of 'civilization'.

But are all developments in information technologies really producing a better society? Has the power of the microprocessor increased our understanding of the world around us, of ourselves? Has the microcomputer given hitherto untapped power to the average citizen? Does the profusion of information technologies mean that we are more in control of our destiny? A growing number of scholars are now arguing that the information age far from increasing our control over our own lives is in fact producing the opposite effect. The generation of more and more information and the efforts of individuals and institutions to assert and exercise control over societal circumstances are becoming increasingly counter-productive. Donald Michael summarizes the argument:

> It is a grand irony of our culture that one of its most basic premises — that more information leads to more knowledge, which in turn leads to more power to control — has turned on itself. Instead, we confront the undeniable fact that more information has led to an ever increasing sense that things are out of control. Information about environmental deterioration, economic disarray, toxic wastes, national security, the dissolution of the family, or the stumbling of the schools all point in the same direction: we are unable to control our society, informally to guide it or formally to regulate it, into performing the way we — any group of 'we's' — would want it to perform. What is more, the more information available, the less people are inclined to assign legitimacy to the institutions or organisations described by information. On the one hand, the information reveals ineptitude in practice and fumblings of purpose if not immoral or illegal actions. On the other hand, information provides the grounds for conflicting interpretation of what is going on and what should be done, thereby deepening the conclusion that nobody really knows what to do or how to control the situation. The consequent endemic distrust and delegitimation in turn undermine efforts to gain

control for attaining desirable ends or even for maintaining reliable norm settings, thereby amplifying the indicators of incompetence. Finally, information in the form of future studies strongly implies that things are highly unlikely to become controllable in the years ahead [1].

The 'information age', therefore, is by no means a blessing. For western society it has produced a whole range of problems the solutions to which are by no means evident. For the Muslim World, the information revolution poses special challenges which have to be met for the sake of the physical and cultural survival of the *ummah*. Not least of these challenges is the primary dilemma: should Muslim countries embrace a compulsive, totalitarian technology and risk inducing a new, more subversive and devastating type of dependency; or should they preserve their meagre and valuable resources, ignore the developments in information technology and leave their destiny in western hands?

The basic assumption of this study is that dealing with the new information technologies is like walking through a mine field. The Muslim countries can neither afford to overlook this important technological development nor can they uncritically, and wholeheartedly, embrace it. Information is rapidly becoming a prime commodity and source of power. In the next few decades, information technologies will become the basic tools of manipulation and control; access to information will become the decisive factor between those who will command real power and those who will simply be manipulated and made to serve as subject people. For the Muslim countries, the information age may well turn out to be a new age of colonialism. The prescriptive elements of this study are designed to avoid just such a possibility.

My main message is that we must understand both the pros and cons of information technology and consciously use it to serve *our* goals, and not those of the makers and creators of the technology. Ideally, we must develop local capability in the generation and use of this technology. But, while all technology comes with the ideology and cultural trappings of the civilization which is responsible for producing it, it is also possible to change and modify it at the point of use. Where we are forced to use the existing technology, it must be modified to suit our needs and requirements.

However, we must develop an overall, well thought-out and informed strategy to deal with the challenges of the information age. Such a strategy, by necessity, must involve an understanding of the nature of information as well as a vision of the society that we wish to create for ourselves. Beyond this, the strategy must serve both individual Muslim countries as well as the Muslim world as a whole, scientists and decision-makers as well as citizens and peasants. Finally, it must assign a specific role to the professional information scientist who has special skills to deal with the complexities of the information age. The strategy presented in this study covers most of this basic ground.

Over three decades of development experience has taught us that much of the information generated in industrialized countries is of little relevance to developing countries. It has now become imperative for the so-called 'Third World' states to develop an infrastructure for generating their own information, to become research-orientated and knowledge-based societies. For Muslim countries this is particularly vital when they are so much concerned with the preservation of their culture and values and when Muslim academics and intellectuals are working to create a whole range of new disciplines — such as Islamic economics and political science, Islamic science and environmental legislation, contemporary modes for the establishment of the *Shariah* and 'Islamization of knowledge' — which are geared to meeting the needs and aspirations of Muslim societies. However, if it becomes necessary to rely on research done elsewhere, to transfer information from one country to another, it is better to choose a country at the same level of development and with similar needs because information generated there is much more likely to be relevant. As such, my suggestions for establishing national information systems and creating mechanisms for the transfer of information are written from this perspective.

Because of certain factors inherent in information technologies, an integrated information strategy for the Muslim world should not rely too exclusively on them. Certain traditional information agencies, such as rural libraries and community information and referral services, have a vital role to play both in providing access to much needed information for citizens and eradicating such dominant ills of Muslim societies as illiteracy and poor sanitation practices. This is why I believe in emphasizing traditional forms of disseminating information. It is my belief that whatever new developments the galloping information technologies may produce, nothing can replace the book and the library: the cornerstone of the Muslim civilization of the classical period. Only by giving these two institutions the respect and the wide currency that they deserve can Muslim civilization regain the position it once held.

The challenges of the new information technologies should be met not with despair or desperate optimism; but with informed and thoughtful action. The strategy outlined in this study is the minimum that we can hope to fulfil. If action is taken to discuss, criticize, improve and implement the strategy outlined here we would have already overcome the first, and perhaps the major hurdle: the inertia and apathy that so dominates the Muslim world.

Notes

1. Donald Michael, 'Competence and Compassion in an Age of Uncertainty', *World Future Society Bulletin*, Jan.–Feb. 1983.

1

Bits and Pieces

Making Sense of Information

The conventional approach to information is based on an analysis of chance events with various possible outcomes. There is no need for me to present the mathematical analysis here. This approach was developed simultaneously in cybernetics and thermodynamics and the mathematical analysis can be found in any standard text on cybernetics and thermodynamics.[1] The essential feature of this approach is the 'atomic' conception of information which emphasizes only the quantitative aspects of information. The qualitative aspects of information, such as cognitive meaning or cultural significance, are either totally ignored or considered to be secondary or accidental.

The over-emphasis on mechanistic and statistical approaches to information has had a devastating effect on society. On the one hand, it has tried to give information a neutral face; and on the other, it has lead to a fragmentation of information from its traditional base of knowledge and wisdom. The former has had a serious impact on technology itself: concentration on quantitative information has been at the expense of quality control, and such hazardous technologies as nuclear power, recombinant-DNA technology and computerized weapons control have escaped even the standard industrial considerations of quality control. The latter process has lead to a dehumanization and alienation of society.

The reductive refinement of the concept of information was a slow, gradual process, extending over several decades. It involved two phases.

The first step in this process was the separation of wisdom from knowledge. This occurred as a divorce between knowledge and values. Consider for a moment the fact that never in the history of mankind has knowledge been pursued on such a vast scale as today, and never has the estrangement of man from this world, and from his fellow men, been greater. Exponential increase in our knowledge seems to bring not enlightenment, but confusion. This is only natural for knowledge without values is nothing but a skeleton, bones without flesh, body without skin.

The second step in this process of reduction has been the translation of knowledge, first into information and then into fragments of information. This has placed knowledge into a vacuum-sealed container; from this container we pick bits of information for the task at hand. As a result there is no longer unity between man and his knowledge. There are only specialized bits of information for specialized tasks. The process is de-humanized, isolated, alienated. We have gradually stepped down from the ladder of wisdom, so that now we stand on the ground level with a foreshortened view of the horizons ahead. The situation is elegantly summed up by T.S. Eliot:

> Where is the wisdom
> We have lost in knowledge?
> Where is the knowledge
> We have lost in information?[2]

The divorce between knowledge and values has given birth to a world where human beings are quantized. When the state of one's knowledge does not allow one to make sense of the world, confusion and extremism become the norms. Witness the paramount confusion evident in the lifestyles and behaviour of American and European youth, and the phenomenal rise of numerous cults, fetishes and fanatical philosophies. When all one has are bits of information, data, and expertise then, of course, one would try to hold on to anything that purports or pretends to give meaning to life and tries to make sense of reality beyond the immediately comprehensible.

This confusion is also evident amongst Muslim youth and intellectuals. Much of the knowledge they acquire turns out to be irrelevant. Their training in disciplines such as economics, sociology, architecture, engineering, biology does not train them to promote the values they cherish nor allow, except in a very limited sense, their individual creativity and cultural consciousness to flower. This is not surprising for these disciplines are more relevant to the occidental capitalist and socialist economic structure, values and norms. It is not only that these systems have no relevance to Islam but also that these systems of economic, ecological and human exploitation are not interested in knowledge as such, only in bits of information and expertise which promote the systems and ensure their smooth running. This is why our universities equip us with information and expertise, not with knowledge. If our young people and intellectuals are in a state of confusion this is because their knowledge is often isolated from their value system. Furthermore, if they were determined, and furnished with knowledge, they might question the validity of the system itself.

It can be argued that information *per se* is neither good nor bad. It is the users who make right or wrong use of information. Science, it is contended, does no harm, the harm derives from the people who apply it. Let us be categorical: there is no such thing as value-free information or data. In the gathering, selection and use of all information and data a value system is in operation — information from occidentalized science is geared to promote the occidental system of values and norms; it serves only the interests of the occident and those who share the occidental world-view. Knowledge and information mould peoples' minds and outlook as much as people mould knowledge and information; how people approach information depends very much on their world-view.

Information: A Multi-Dimensional Phenomenon

The reductive world-view of modern natural and social sciences emphasizes only the 'neutral', objective aspects of information. However, as Ronald Benge points out, information, as distinct from bits of information, is a process which includes personal and social components. Benge explains this assertion as follows:

> If a document should lie (as many of them do) quite lost in some attic, can this be regarded as information? It is *unused* information. Once it is discovered or retrieved it can be of value. But the meaning lies in the use. You may call a spade a spade but if it is being wielded as a weapon rather than employed for digging, does it not have a different significance? We must assume that a document does not contain information for illiterate persons. Similarly if it is written in a lost language, it becomes a scrap of paper. We are suggesting, therefore, that the meaning of information cannot be understood without reference to its social function.

We would, however, go a step further: information is generated and has real meaning and significance within a social milieu. Social function does not only make sense of information, it is also the reason why information is generated. If, for example, we write the sequence

discrete facts — data — information — theory — world-view

we can see that the participation of subjectivity and human erudition increases as we move to the right of the sequence. However, the left-most end of the spectrum, data or discrete facts, is not entirely independent of human choice and intentions. It is within a world-view that information is generated and the ultimate aim of any information is to promote the world-view responsible for its production. Information, however 'objective' it is assumed to be, cannot be separated from the value system and the cultural concerns of its producers.

As a multi-dimensional phenomenon, we can identify six components of information: absolute; substitutional; philosophic; subjective; cultural; objective. The first branch of the information tree refers to the type of information which is taken for granted and requires no explanation. The second branch refers to cases when the concept of information is used for an amount of information; here 'communication' or 'variety' are sometimes substituted for information. The third branch is concerned with the concepts that relate information to knowledge and wisdom. The fourth branch relates information to human feelings and emotions, the extent to which information depends on man. The fifth branch refers to the logical character of certain types of information, and finally, the sixth branch emphasizes the cultural dimension of information.

All these components of information are interlinked and inter-dependent. One's cultural outlook, to give an example, would determine what one considers to be absolute information. To a Muslim, for instance, his values and norms are absolute, to a proponent of mass–culture only the technologically–dependent values have absolute meaning. One's absolute information would be a measure of reflection, and a tool in obtaining philosophic information. Yet again, those who take the objective as the absolute, may not even recognize the existence, let alone the value, of subjective and cultural information.

These aspects of information are generated within the matrix of societal knowledge which acts as a guide and provides a mapping of human life and environment. Societal knowledge is influenced by four types of informing systems which shape its nature and character. The first of these is the *weltanschauung*, or world-view. It is the broadest of informing systems and links cosmology to ethics and can be theistic or non–theistic in orientation. Its sources include the Qur'an, the Bible, the Upanishads, the teachings of Buddha, the writings of Marx, and the myths of classical Greece and Polynesia. These sources reduce to conceptually manageable and predictable quantities a person's everyday information overload. A second kind of societal knowledge is nationalism. Nationalism is narrower than world-view; people incorporate the supremacy of national individuality in their scale of social values through such emotions as national pride, political loyalty, ethnic unity and patriotism. It is an informing system that arranges information into effective units such as loyalty and common consciousness and relates a person to his common language and social and political environment. The third type of informing system relates to societal institutions. Institutions such as the family, or business organizations, generate values which give priority to this or that type of information. Personal philosophy is the fourth and the final type of informing system. Here we are not concerned with psychological roots but the self-conscious aspects of an individual's personality. Personal philosophy allows people to acquire and redefine their views of reality and their axiological orientations in matters of ethics, justice and taste. Personal philosophy acts as a gauge by which an individual monitors his natural and social environment in real space/time terms. These four informing systems shape societal knowledge; and information is generated within the matrix of societal knowledge. Thus the generation of information is dictated by the demands of the world-view, real or perceived needs of the nation–state, requirements of social and organizational institutions of society, and personal outlook. And it is these informing systems that the generated information ultimately serves.

Thus information can never be 'neutral'; it has been created within certain boundaries to serve definite national, organizational or personal needs. Once created it carries with it all of its six components, the information tree, as well as all branches of contemporary sciences, natural and social, as well as technologies. No matter how objective or 'neutral' a particular discipline is made out to be, it has its subjective elements that interact with the cultural and philosophic components of information. Indeed, as I have argued extensively elsewhere, disciplines themselves have real meaning only in a particular world-view and have emerged to fulfil particular national needs. A great deal of contemporary literature on the dynamics between science and society, particularly that based on Marxist and radical analysis, highlights the subjective and cultural aspects of supposedly objective and neutral information.

Thus when dealing with information we must be aware of its true nature. We must be cognizant of the informing systems which were involved in its creation as well as its subjective and cultural load. Indeed, any definition of information for the purpose of our analysis must incorporate these aspects of information. But such a definition of information would require a great deal of manoeuvre, hedging every phrase with qualification and a rather generous supply of string and bees' wax. As such, I offer not so much a definition but more a way of looking at information: Information is a multi-dimensional proposition(s) with absolute, and objective as well as subjective and cultural components, extracted, deductively or inductively, from raw data gathered, selected and organized on the basis of a world-view, national needs, institutional demands and/or personal philosophy to increase its usefulness in decision-making, planning and goal-seeking actions. The methods used for processing the data and concepts for its analysis are geared to achieve this condition. The emphasis here is on the subjective nature of information and the value-dependency of the methodology and conceptual analysis of all types of research and information work. A 'bit' of information now becomes an elementary idea. A system which processes information — collects, thinks, acts and decides — must now be looked on as a total system.

It is obvious that in this notion information becomes useful only when it is integrated with societal knowledge. Only when it is seen within the context of its generation and use does it become meaningful. In the context of the Muslim world, information has true meaning when it is generated within the knowledge base of Muslim society or, when it has to be transferred, is integrated and synthesized with the world-view of Islam. Information makes a positive contribution to society when it exists in complete synthesis with societal knowledge and cultural wisdom. Without this integration and synthesis, it becomes a burden on society, and could result in disintegration and fragmentation of both society and the minds of individuals.

However, from the perspective of the Muslim world, and developing countries, we need to realize not just that information has strong subjective, cultural and world-view components, but also that it has now assumed the garb of a commodity; and in the near future could become a major means of control and domination.

Information: Commodity and Control

To appreciate the emergence of information as a commodity, and the possible manipulation of this commodity for imperialistic ends, it is necessary to understand the role of information in the decision-making process. We can illustrate how information assists decision-making, including the political decision-making process, by using the general model of information flow of Yovits, Rose and Abilock.[4] This model of a generalized information system is based on three assumptions: information is data of value in decision-making; information gives rise to observable effects; and information feedback exists so that the decision-maker will adjust this model for later similar decisions. To solve a problem, a decison-maker tries to meet two main objectives: to choose the 'best' course of action according to a given criteria and state of knowledge; and to learn as much as possible about the total existing situation from the decision-making process. Yovits *et al* suggest that a decision-maker learns about a particular situation and the environment by a cyclic process of the following type:

1. He makes a decision on the basis of available information;
2. He predicts some probable outcomes;
3. He compares actual resulting observables against his predicted observables;
4. He updates his total model of the existing situation as a result of this process; and
5. He repeats the cycle. (Figure 1.1)

Figure 1.1   Decision-making environment

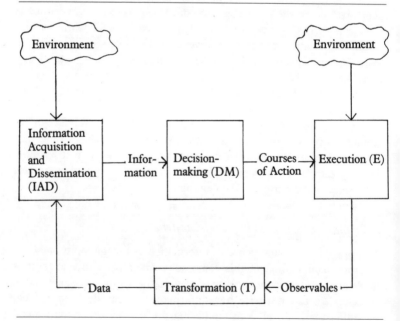

Even in this rather primitive model, the role of information in reducing the uncertainties with which the decision-maker must cope is quite explicit. In fact, Yovits *et al* discuss the value of information in terms of 'decision-maker effectiveness', and develop two matrices which measure information amount and information value. While information amount is concerned with the change in a decision-maker's plans for dealing with a particular situation, information value defines the value accrued from the decision-maker's change in probabilities. The two measures are distinct but interdependent.

During the last few decades, developed economies have slowly been turning into information economies. For example, in the United States the role of information began to gain importance during the period 1945 to 1965, when mechanization and automation were increased in a number of fields. From 1960, the role of information in the American economy increased slowly with various kinds of mechanization and automation in banking and credit, office work, record-keeping and data storage and retrieval. By the mid-seventies, more people were employed in the manipulation of information than were employed in mining, agriculture, manufacturing and personal services combined. By the early eighties, Peter Druker has estimated, 52 per cent of the US GNP was related to information.[5] This figure is increasing rapidly and many economists are now beginning to consider information as the key commodity of developed economies.

However, the role of information in developing economies has not been studied. In contrast, the value of information in political decision-making has been studied quite extensively by political scientists. Also considerable attention has been paid in political science and mass communication to the potential of mass media for creating a decision structure in the developing countries and helping Third World nations reach their development goals. But the study of information flows in the Third World environment and its impact on the political, social, economic and cultural goals of the developing countries has been largely overlooked in information science.

However, in the environment of the developing countries, where political uncertainties dominate and the complex web of social and cultural problems add to the burden of dependent economies, information needs of the decision-makers can be assumed to be much more acute than for their counterparts in industrialized countries. If it was possible to control the flow of information — across the whole area of society, from industry to education, politics to early warning signals of approaching disasters — to decision-makers in the Muslim world, then the organization of a whole state could be controlled. Thus the control of information is the key to the leverage and political subversion of a developing country.

The developing countries have not been oblivious to the growing importance of information as a tool for command and domination. Witness the fact that the demand for a new international economic order by the Third World was soon followed by a specific demand for a new international order of information. Witness also how this demand has been resisted by the industrialized countries; to the extent of weakening and threatening the destruction of UNESCO. Indeed, the importance of information in reshaping the world economic, scientific and technological order cannot be underestimated.

The simplest type of economic analysis of information distinguishes four components in information: commodity, process, state of knowing, and environment. The concept of *commodity* is intended to capture empiricist notions of information. As a commodity, information represents something, some event, some state of mind. The *process* component is supposed to capture the formalist and objective notion of information. Here the structural and organizational aspects of information are emphasized. As a process, information is represented by something, some generic structure, for example. The *state of knowing* component relates information to the change it produces on the recipient. Here information transfer is being equated with communication; a point which is debatable. And finally, if information is considered as a system it must have an *environment*. The concept of environment is used largely in information system analysis, and refers to man–machine and man–man systems within which certain information transfer occurs.[6]

This type of information analysis has led much of information science research to resemble the development work attached to the processes of a new consumer industry. The firm is seen as a learning system within a unique situation and the methodology of market research is wholeheartedly adopted for repeated identification of new groups of users and their needs, for discerning channels for dissemination of information and the investigations of acceptability of new information services. Thus information science is itself growing as a science which is shaped by 'market forces' with its ultimate ideological bias in the direction of those who control the market.

Just as nation-states today fight for control of resources and over commodity prices, in the not-too-distant future, information, as a commodity indispensable to productive power, will become the stake in the world-wide competition for power. Lyotard warns,

It is conceivable that the nation-states will one day fight for control of information, just as they battled in the past for control over territory, and afterwards for control of access to and exploitation of raw materials and cheap labour. A new field is opened for industrial and commercial strategies on the one hand, and political and military strategies on the other.[7]

What would be the role of information science in this 'new field'? Given the contemporary trends in industrialized countries, the importance of information would not simply stop at the level of its being treated as a commodity. If, as has been argued by a number of writers, the economy is an information system and involves flows of information,[8] then the next step would require information to assume the same role as money. Just as in modern monetarized economies, money is used to make more money and generate wealth, in information economies information would be used to generate wealth. Information would be bought for investment. Indeed, there would emerge a whole group of people who would simply buy and sell information for profit. Given the fact that information science is evolving according to market criteria, the information scientist of the future could easily become a highly specialized form of stock broker dealing in 'payment information' and 'investment information'.

Given the trend that information is rapidly acquiring the same importance as capital, and that both information science and the technologies associated with it could become new and frighteningly powerful tools of neo-imperialism, what can Muslim countries do to prepare themselves to meet this challenge?

Towards an Information Strategy for the Muslim World

From an Islamic perspective, the first thing to realize is that information has significance only within a framework of societal knowledge; only when its objective component is in harmony with absolute, substitutional, cultural and subjective aspects of a society does information make a positive contribution to that society. Such harmony can evolve only when Muslim states generate their own information with the relevant apparatus geared to meeting the needs of their decision-makers and communities. An information strategy for the Muslim world has to be based on this realization.

The Muslim scholars of the classical period knew well that when information is divorced from its cultural and value context, it becomes meaningless. Indeed, much of my understanding of the connection between information, knowledge and wisdom derives from the classification schemes of such scholars as al-Farabi, ibn Sina, al-Ghazzali and ibn Khaldun. These scholars knew that discrete facts, or 'bits' of information, are not gathered in isolation; they have meaning only within a framework of societal knowledge, and when two are synthesized in an enlightened manner, the outcome is wisdom.

An excellent illustration of this occurs in the *Mathnavi* of Maulana Jala-ud-din-Rumi where an anecdote of four cosmopolitan friends who came across a lost coin is related.[9] The first being a Persian, declared 'I will buy with this some *angur*.' The second being an Arab, insisted 'No, we should buy some *inab*.' The third was a Turk. He said 'I do not want *inab*, I want *uzum*.' The fourth was a Greek, he confessed that he was not interested in any of the other suggestions: 'I want *stafili*,' he said.

Maulana Rumi tells us that because the four friends did not know what lay behind the names of things, they started to fight. They had information but no knowledge. It so happened that a man of wisdom passed by. He reconciled the friends, saying 'I can fulfil the needs of all of you with one and the same coin if you honestly give me your trust. Your one coin will become as four and four at odds will become as one united.'

The man then bought some grapes for the quarrelsome friends, and they were all delighted. For each, in his own language, had expressed the desire for the same thing, grapes.

On the part of Maulana Rumi, the anecdote is a clear attempt to differentiate between the three concepts of information, knowledge and wisdom. Information is characterized here as the desire of the four friends to eat *angur, inab, uzum* and *stafili*. This desire can be expressed as unorganized and unrelated statements of facts. The wise man could arrange these facts into an organized body of information because of his knowledge; and his wisdom enabled him to apply this knowledge, with information thoroughly assimilated, to produce sound judgement and enlightened insight.

Any information strategy for the Muslim world must attempt to place information within the context of societal knowledge and traditional wisdom. We seem to have particular difficulty in understanding and appreciating the latter quality. Yet, in the present state of the Muslim world with a vast array of complex, interrelated problems, and more generally, considering the condition of mankind, confronted with exponentially increasing crises, nothing could be more fatal than the lack of wisdom. The *Shorter Oxford Dictionary* gives a general definition of wisdom as 'the capacity of judging rightly in matters relating to life and conduct; soundness of judgement in the choice of means and ends;

sometimes, less strictly, sound sense, especially in practical affairs.'[10] Of the quality of sound judgement, the Prophet of Islam said, 'A word of wisdom which man learns is better for him than the world and all that is in it.'

We have to turn to classical Muslim scholars for a true appreciation of this quality. The Arabic word for wisdom is *hikma*. Of *hikma* al-Ghazzali says that when knowledge is rightly developed and becomes perfect, it is *hikma*. Knowledge can be praiseworthy or blameworthy but *hikma* can distinguish the true from the false in judgements, the right from the wrong in beliefs, and the good from the evil in actions. Al-Ghazzali gives four manifestations of wisdom:

1. *Husn at tadbir* (administrative ability). This ability enables one to find the best way of achieving good for oneself or for others, e.g., in the administration of the state or the family, or in overcoming enemies or evil. This virtue is exercised particularly in momentous affairs. When wisdom is exercised in matters of little significance, it is distinguished from *husn at tadbir* and is called *kais* (tact).
2. *Fawdat adh-dhihan* (acute-mindedness). The ability which helps in arriving at the correct decision when opinions are divided.
3. *Naqayat ar-rae* (clearness of vision) is the insight which helps one to adopt the right means for achieving the best results for a given problem.
4. *Sawab az-zaha* (shrewdness) is the ability to discover the subtle points in thought or action and to accept truth straightaway on the evidence of experience without getting into fallacious arguments about it.[11] From these manifestations of wisdom, it is clear that this quality implies the ability to discriminate between different options, modes of thought and varieties of actions relevant to particular applications and situations. Both content of thought and decisions for action can be related to the framework of knowledge and the phenomena of information.

The Muslim philosophers have seen the whole continuum of discrete facts, information, knowledge, and wisdom in terms of a hierarchy with wisdom at the top of the ladder and discrete facts at the bottom. It was generally accepted that there was a relationship between these concepts. Each step up the ladder required a process of selection, decision and synthesis. The whole process was seen through the value system of Islam, and it was recognized that each of the first three steps of the ladder could lead man to praiseworthy activities.

A contemporary information strategy for the Muslim world must seek to integrate information with knowledge and wisdom and place it within the matrix of the world-view of Islam. We can achieve this if we make the generation and dissemination of information subject to some of the basic values and aspects of the Islamic *weltanschauung*. It is the world-view of a society which determines its absolute, philosophic and cultural outlook; it provides the ethical criteria which determine and direct behaviour and generation and distribution of objective knowledge.

At least seven concepts of the world-view of Islam have a direct hearing on the generation and dissemination of information: *tawheed* (unity of God), *ilm* (knowledge), *hikma* (wisdom), *adl* (justice), *ijma* (consensus), *shura* (consultation), *istislah* (public interest) and *umah* (the world-wide Muslim community).

The notion of *tawheed* demands that Muslim societies do not get in a position where they are forced to bow down to outside powers. Independence in information therefore is the first ethical criteria of the world-view of Islam. Dependency negates *tawheed*; thus it becomes a moral responsibility for Muslim societies to develop indigenous capability to deal with information. However, creations and distribution of information has to be carried out within the framework of *ilm*: to promote praiseworthy knowledge information should fulfil the needs of society, that is, it should serve the dictates of *istislah*, public interest, and promote *hikma* — a vision of a dynamic, thriving Muslim civilization with ability, shrewdness and acute-mindedness. It should, reflecting the ultimate characteristic of the Creator, promote all round unity bringing the Muslim world together, integrating knowledge and values, and uniting the Muslim community with nature and the natural environment. Information processes should promote *adl*: that is information should be sought by just means and distributed justly so that all those who need access to it have the means to acquire it. It should promote the politics of *ijma* and *shura*: before people can be consulted they must have assimilated the relevant information; and consensus can be reached only when all facts of a particular policy are known. To protect the interest of the public at large, that is to guard *istislah*, all information on matters which affect an average citizen, his heatlh, his environment, must be openly and readily available.

An information strategy which is guided by a matrix of basic Islamic concepts would have a profound impact on Muslim societies. Apart from healing the Muslim civilization and providing it with a new impetus to reconstruct itself, it will provide new mechanisms for putting into operation some of the most important, but hitherto dormant, Islamic concepts. For example, the question of unity: an information network which links the Muslim world, say on the lines of Euronet, will increase interaction amongst Muslims, reduce misunderstanding and mutual suspicions, and hence pave the way for true unity and integration of the Muslim world: it will give true significance to the notion of the *ummah*. Take another example: the oft-cited but seldom practised notion of *ijma*. The essential thing about information is that it has a surprise value. It can lead to decision. If there are no choices or decisions, information would be unnecessary. The decisions can range from the simple, repetitive, to long-range strategic ones. We cannot judge information for value unless we know the decision affected by it. And more than that: decisions are not taken in isolation. Every decision must be part of a *decision structure*. Now a network of rural and urban libraries and community information centres can play a very important part in evolving a decision structure — facilities for reaching a consensus, an *ijma* within a society. Many cherished Islamic concepts cannot be realized because they do not have an institutional base: Muslim societies have lost the social, economic, political and cultural institutions which traditionally promoted these conceptual values. The implementation of an information strategy based on these values would create newer and more relevent institutions for their support.

Notes

1. See, for example, the classic works of Norbert Wiener, *Cybernetics or Control and Communication in Animals and Machines*, MIT Press, Cambridge, Massachusetts, 1948; and Leon Brioleon, *Science and Information Theory*, Paris, 1949.
2. T.S. Eliot, Chorus I, The Rock, *Selected Poems*, Faber and Faber, London, 1954.
3. Ronald C. Benge, *Cultural Crisis and Libraries in the Third World*, Clive Bingley, London, 1979, p. 191.
4. M.C. Yovits, L. Rose and J. Abilock, 'Development of a theory of information flow and analysis' in *Many Faces of Information Science*, E.C. Weiss (ed.), Westview Press, Colorado, 1977.
5. Peter Druker, *Managing in Turbulent Times*, Harper and Row, New York, 1981, p. 48.
6. A number of authors have carried out such analysis, see for example, M.U. Porat, *The Information Economy*, vols. 1-9, Office of Telecommunications, US Department of Commerce, 1977; D. Mc Lamberton (ed.), *Economics of Information and Knowledge*, Penguin, London, 1971; and H. A. Olsen, *Economics of Information: Bibliography and Commentry on the Literature* American Society for Information Science, Washington, D.C., 1971.
7. Jean-Francois Lyotard, *The Post-Modern Condition: A Report on Knowledge*, Manchester University Press, 1986, p. 5.

8. See for example, F. R. Hutin, 'Informatics is a Political Issue', *Intermedia* 9(1):17–19, 1981; A. Madec, 'The Political Economy of Information Flows', *Intermedia* 9(2):29–32 (1981); and A. Mattelart, 'Infotech and the Third World', *Radical Science*, **16** 27–35 (1985).

9. This and other tales of wisdom can be found in *Teachings of Rumi: The Masnavi*, abridged and translated by E. H. Whinfield, The Octagon Press, London, 1973.

10. C.J. Onions (ed.), *The Shorter Oxford Dictionary in Historical Principles*, 3rd ed., Oxford University Press, 1968, p. 2436.

11. Al-Ghazzali, Mizan al-Amal, quoted by Muhammad Umaruddin, *The Ethical Philosophy of al Ghazzali*, Ashraf, Lahore, 1962; cf: Al-Ghazzali, *The Book of Knowledge*, Nabih Amin Faris (trans.), Ashraf, Lahore, 1962; and ibn Khaldun, *The Muqaddimah: An Introduction to History*, F. Rozenthal (trans.), Routledge and Kegan Paul, London, 1967.

2

Past and Present

Going Forward to the Islamic Heritage

When the basic concepts of the Islamic world-view are actualized in all their sophistication at various levels of society and civilization, they yield an integrated infrastructure for the distribution of knowledge. At least five Islamic concepts have a direct bearing on the distribution of information: *adl* (justice), *ilm* (knowledge), *ibadah* (worship), *khalifa* (trusteeship) and *waqf* (pious endowment; charitable trust). An examination of the early history of Islam reveals how these five concepts were given practical shape and generated a highly sophisticated infrastructure for the distribution of information and knowledge.

The all-embracing concept of *ilm* shaped the outlook of the Muslim people right from the beginning of Islam. Islam actually made the pursuit of knowledge a religious obligation: by definition, to be a Muslim is to be deeply entrenched in generation, production, processing and dissemination of knowledge. Moreover, the concept of *ilm* is not a limiting or elitist notion. *Ilm* is distributive knowledge: it is not a monopoly of individual, class, group or sex; it is not an obligation only for a few, freeing the vast majority of the society; it is not limited to a particular field of inquiry or discipline but covers all dimensions of human awareness and the entire spectrum of natural phenomena. Indeed, Islam places *ilm* at par with *adl*: the pursuit of knowledge is as important as the pursuit of justice. Just as *adl* is essentially distributive justice, so is *ilm* distributive knowledge. One is an instrument for achieving the other. The ideal goal of the world-view of Islam, establishment of a just and equitable society, cannot be achieved without the instrument of distributive knowledge. Only when knowledge is widely and easily available to all segments of society can justice be established in its Islamic manifestations.

Early Muslim communities were well aware of this interconnection of *adl* and *ilm*. To begin with they faced the question of distributing the Qur'an and the traditions of the Prophet amongst the believers. Only when the believers had access to copies of the Qur'an and authentic collections of the hadith could they be expected to behave according to their dictates. The first steps in this direction were taken by Uthman, the third Caliph of Islam. He was aware that the phenomenon of total memorization of the Qur'an, and its preservation in the hearts and minds of the believers, was indeed a manifestation of the distributive notion of *ilm*. Because the Qur'an could be easily memorized, its contents could be just as easily distributed. Nevertheless, in view of the variations of dialects, he felt it necessary to preserve it in a written form. As such he took the necessary steps for the preservation of the written text. The next step was taken by the compilers of hadith who evolved a sophisticated process of authenticating the traditions and made them widely available to all segments of society.

During the first century of Islam, oral traditions predominated and were the chief vehicle for the dissemination of information. But it soon became clear that memory could not be relied upon completely; and written notes began to circulate amongst the seekers of knowledge. Thus, we hear from Sa'd ibn Jubair (d. 714): 'In the lectures of ibn Abbas, I used to write on my page; when it was filled, I wrote on the upper leather of my shoes, and then on my hand'; and 'My father used to say to me, "Learn by heart, but attend above all to writing, when you come home from lectures write, and if you fall into need or your memory fails you, you have your books".'[1]

What did ibn Jubair actually take his notes on? His page was probably papyrus made from the stem of a plant of the same name or a parchment prepared from the skins of goats. Notes gathered like that were freely exchanged amongst students and scholars. Indeed, quite often such notes were combined to form books. Evidence from ibn Ishaq, al-Wakidi, ibn Sa'd, al-Baladhuri, at-Tabari and al-Bukhari suggests that Urwa ibn al-Zubair (d. 712–13) was the first to collect such loose-leaf books. And his student, al-Zuhri (d. 742) collected so many that his house had space for few other things. His preoccupation with collecting and studying books occupied so much of his time that his wife was led to complain: 'By Allah! These books annoy me more than three other wives would (if you had them).' Ruth Stellhorn Mackensen, who during the early forties carried out a pioneering study of the emergence of Muslim libraries, considers al-Zahri's collection as the first Muslim library. She notes: 'Whether the early books were merely collection of students' notes and little treatise in the form of letters or more formal books, of which there were at least a few, the collecting of them, the recognition that such materials were worth keeping, can legitimately be considered the beginning of Muslim libraries.'[2]

But even during this period, the book — as a coherent record of thoughts — had emerged. Indeed, noted men of learning were commissioned to write books and they were encouraged to do so by students who wished their lecture notes to be transformed into coherent form. Al-Amash abu Mohammed Sulaiman ibn Mihran (680–765), a fiercely independent and witty scholar of tradition was frequently approached to write books. Not all the commissions he received were worthy of his attention. When Caliph Hisham ibn Abd Allah wrote asking him to compose a book on the virtues of Caliph Uthman and the crimes of Caliph Ali, al-Amash read the note and thrust it into the mouth of a sheep, which ate it up, and said to the messenger, 'Tell him I answer it thus.' When a few students arrived at his house early one day and insisted that he teach them some traditions, he eventually came out. After greeting them, he announced, 'Were there not in the house a person [meaning his wife] whom I detest more than I do you, I would not have come out to you.'[3]

By the time al-Amash died the book had become a common and widely used vehicle for the distribution of knowledge and information. This was largely due to the emergence of paper. The Muslims learnt the art of paper making from the Chinese. When Muslims came into contact with the Chinese in the latter part of the seventh century — a direct outcome of Prophet Mohammad saying, 'Go in quest of knowledge even unto China' — they quickly realized the role paper could play in the distribution of knowledge. The first Muslim town to set up a paper industry was Samarkand. It came into Muslim possession in 704; and Thaalibi in his *Lata'if al-maarif*[4] and Qazwini in his *Athar al-Bilad*[5] tell us that the paper industry of Samarkand was established by Chinese prisoners of war. From there the industry soon spread to the central provinces and major cities of the Muslim empire: Samarkand was responsible for setting up the paper industry of Baghdad, from whence it proceeded to Damascus, then Cairo, Fez and Cordova. In a matter of decades, paper displaced papyrus and parchment and became the main medium for the dissemination of written information. Indeed, the new industry flourished so well that by the end of the century parchment was replaced with paper for government documents.

Along with paper manufacturing, other industries connected with the production of the book also developed rapidly. The preparation of ink in various colours, and the technology of writing and illustrating instruments, advanced considerably during this period. Bookbinding too acquired a considerable degree of sophistication. Originally the bindings were rather crude: books were bound in rough leather and dressed in lime; the binding remained stiff and hard. However, a discovery in Kufa led to a more effective way of dressing leather. This was done using dates and produced softer and limper leather. At the same time, new skills for the ornamentation of bindings and techniques for the illumination of books were developed. The overall result was a book which was not only breathtaking to look at but was also a real work of art. Even the oldest Arab bindings that have come down to us have tasteful designs pressed into the rim and central shields; they are simple but have an elegance and beauty of their own.[6] Books produced at later dates contain splendid decorations and lovingly executed illuminations in a kaleidoscope of colours.[7]

Thus just over a hundred years after the advent of Islam, the book industry had been nurtured to such an extent that the Muslims became the 'people of the book' in the truest sense; and reading, not just the 'Noble Reading' (the Qur'an), became one of the major occupations and pastimes. The connection between reading and the Qur'an is important: it enforces the notion that the pursuit of knowledge is a form of worship, that *ilm* and *ibadah* are two faces of the same coin.

It was hardly surprising then that in the next two centuries, the book industry spread to every corner of the Muslim world. Libraries — royal, public, specialized, private; bookshops — small, adjacent to mosques, large, in the centre of cities, in collectives in special sections of the bazaars; and bookmen — authors, translators, copiers, illuminators, librarians, booksellers and collectors — were all aspects of Muslim civilization that revolved around the book. Listen to Ibn Jammah, writing in 1273 in his *Books as the Tools of the Scholars*:

> Books are needed in all useful scholarly pursuits. A student, therefore, must in every possible manner try to get hold of them. He must try to buy, or hire, or borrow them, since these are the ways to get hold of them. However, the acquisition, collection, and possession of books in great numbers should not become the student's only claim to scholarship . . . Do not bother with copying books that you can buy. It is more important to spend your time studying books than copying them. And do not be content with borrowing

books that you can buy or hire. . . . The lending of books to others is recommendable, if no harm to either borrower or lender is involved. Some people disapprove of borrowing books, but the other attitude is the more correct and preferable one, since lending something to someone else is in itself a meritorious action and, in the case of books, in addition serves to promote knowledge.[8]

Lending of books became a vogue throughout the Muslim world. Libraries were built in almost every major town. To begin with, there were the magnificent royal libraries of the caliphs. Almost every dynasty, from the Ummayad and Abbasid Caliphs, to the Umayyads of Spain, the Fatimids of Egypt, the Hamdanids of Aleppo, the Buwayhids of Persia, the Samanids of Bukhara, the Ghaznavid rulers and the Moghals of India — established major libraries in their respective seats of government.

Libraries and their Management

According to George Makdisi, six terms were used in combination to designate libraries. Three of these denoted locales: *bait* (room), *khizana* (closet), and *dar* (house); and three related to content: *hikma* (wisdom), *ilm* (knowledge) and *kutub* (books). These words and concepts were combined to form seven terms representing libraries: *bait al-hikma, khizanat al-hikma, dar al-hikma, dar al-ilm, dar al-kutub, khizanat al-kutub* and *bait al-kutub*. Two others may be added: *bait al-ilm* and *al-khizana al-ilmiya*. All possible combinations of these were in fact used and often these terms were interchangeable.[9]

Undoubtedly the most famous of the Muslim libraries was the *Bait al-Hikma*, a combination of research institute, library and translation bureau, founded by the Abbasid caliph Harun ar-Rashid in Baghdad in 830. Many of the translations from non-Arabic languages such as Greek and Sanskrit which graced this library are listed in Ibn an-Nadim's *Fihrist* and Haji Khalifah's *Kashf*. Harun ar-Rashid's son, Caliph Mamun ar-Rashid, is reported to have employed scholars of the stature of al-Kindi, the first Muslim philosopher, to translate Aristotle's works into Arabic. Al-Kindi himself wrote nearly 300 books on subjects ranging from medicine and philosophy to music which were stored in the *Bait al-Hikma*. Mamun generously rewarded the translators and as an incentive sealed and signed every translation. Mamun also sent many of his men to distant places, India, Syria, Egypt, to collect rare and unique volumes. The famous physician Hunain ibn Ishaq travelled to Palestine in search of *Kitab al-Burhan*. *Bait al-Hikma* had a number of famous Muslim and non-Muslim scholars on its staff: Qusta ibn Luqa, Yahya ibn Adi, and the Indian physician Duban, to name a few. Musa al-Khwarizmi, the illustrious Muslim mathematician and founder of algebra, also worked at *Bait al-Hikma* and wrote his celebrated book *Kitab al-Jabr wa al-Muqabilah* there. *Bait al-Hikma* continued as *the* library of the Muslim world until the twelfth century. It was only overshadowed by the emergence of Baghdad's second library which boasted a collection of equal quality.

This was the library at the Nizamiyyah Madrassah, founded in 1065 by Nizam al-Mulk, who was a prime-minister in the government of Saljuq Malik Shah. The collection at the Nizamiyyah library was gathered largely through donations: for example, the historian Ibn al-Athir tells us that Muhib ad-Din ibn an-Najjar al-Baghdadi bequeathed his two large personal collections to the library. Caliph an-Nasir donated thousands of books from his royal collection. Among the famous visitors to this library was Nizam al-Mulk at-Tusi (d. 1092) whose book on international law, *Siyar al-Muluk* remains a classic. At-Tusi, during his visits to Baghdad, spent a lot of time at the Nizamiyyah. Nizamiyyah employed regular librarians on its staff who received attractive salaries. Some of the famous librarians of Nizamiyyah included Abu Zakariyyah at-Tibrizi and Yaqub ibn Sulaiman al-Askari. In 1116, the library survived a huge fire and a new building was erected under instructions from Khalifah an-Nasir.

Still in Baghdad, Khalifah Mustansir Billah established an exceptional library at the magnificent madrassah he founded in 1227. Madrassah Mustanriyah, whose ruins are still extant on the banks of the Tigris, also had a hospital attached to it. The library served both the madrassah as well as the hospital. The famous globe-trotter Ibn Battutah has provided a vivid description of Mustanriyah and its library. Through donations, some 150 camel-loads of rare books were donated to this library from the royal holdings alone, the Mustanriyah library acquired a collection of 80,000 volumes.

But Baghdad was not unique in boasting magnificent libraries. Almost every major city in the Muslim world had a library worthy of being called *bait al-hikma* or *dar al-ilm*. Cairo, for example, housed the *Khazain al-Qusu*, the splendid library founded by the Fatimid ruler al-Aziz ibn al-Muizz. In some forty rooms, over 1.6 million books were stored using a sophisticated system of classification. Cairo also boasted a *bait al-hikma* which was established by al-Hakim, the sixth Fatimid caliph, during 1005. It had a hugh collection, including the personal collection of the Caliph. It was open to the general public and free

writing materials were provided to all; those who wished to spend time
for study also received lodgings, meals, and a stipend. But caliphs were
not the only patrons of libraries. Lesser monarchs also contributed to
setting up libraries. For example, the library of Nuh ibn Mansur, the
Sultan of Bokhara, is described by the great philosopher and man of
medicine, Ibn Sina in the following words:

> Having requested and obtained the permission from Nuh ibn Mansur to visit
> the library, I went there and found a great number of rooms filled with books
> packed up in trunks. One room contained philological and poetical works;
> another jurisprudence, and so on, the books on each particular science being
> kept in a room by themselves. I then read the catalogue of the ancient authors
> and found therein all I required. I saw many books the very title of which
> were unknown to most persons, and others which I never met with before or
> since.

When Nuh ibn Mansur offered the premiership of Samarkand to the
scholar Sahib ibn Abbad, he declined stating that it would require 400
camels to transport his books to Samarkand. The Sultan understood the
difficulty and accepted his apology. Like Nuh ibn Mansur, most
regional rulers of that period were great bibliophiles. The library of
Adud ad-Dawlah, for example, was administered by a large staff and
impressed the famous geographer al-Makdisi, who has left a detailed
description of it. It survived till the time of al-Hariri (d.1122).

As they were considered a trust from God, the central libraries were
completely at the disposal of the public; as such they were truly public
libraries. They were open to people from all backgrounds and classes
who had permission to read and freely copy any manuscript they liked.
Moreover, these libraries were not just storehouses of books, but working libraries in every sense. Apart from intensive research programmes,
they were also centres for discussion, lectures, debates and other intellectual public activities. Scholars borrowed books freely and copied
manuscripts. Many of the manuscripts in the celebrated book of the
tenth-century bibliophile, al-Nadim, were copied from the *bait al-
hikma* — a point that has confused many orientalists who have suggested that al-Nadim's *al-Fihrist* [10], which cites over 60,000 books, may
actually be the catalogue of the House of Wisdom.

A considerable amount of thought was given to the design, layout and
architecture to ensure that the public had easy access to books and
appropriate facilities to study and copy manuscripts in the library. Most
of these libraries, like those of Shiraz, Cairo and Cordova were housed in
specially designed buildings of their own, with many rooms for different

purposes, galleries with shelves in which books were kept, rooms where the visitors could sit and read books, and rooms for public lectures and debates, including, in some cases, rooms for musical entertainment. All rooms were richly and comfortably fitted with carpets and mats on which the reader could sit. Heavy curtains created a pleasant atmosphere and maintained the rooms at an appropriate temperature. The description provided by the historian Yaqut of the library of Adud al-Dawlah in Shiraz, provides a general impression of the layout of these institutions:

> The library consists of one large vaulted room, annexed to which are store rooms. The prince had made along the large room the store chambers, scaffoldings about the height of a man, three yards wide, of decorated wood which have shelves from top to bottom; the books are arranged on the shelves and for every branch of learning there are separate scaffolds. There are also catalogues in which all the titles of the books are entered.[11]

Larger libraries like the *bait al-hikma* of Baghdad had separate rooms for copiers, binders and librarians. In his extensive survey *Some Leading Muslim Libraries of the World*, S.M. Imamuddin demonstrates that historic Muslim libraries were designed in 'such a way that the whole library was visible from one central point'.[12] The users thus had open access to the books.

The books in these libraries were not arranged simply according to subject matter. They were properly classified. With the development of books and libraries, and the associated advancement of knowledge, numerous classification schemes appeared. Indeed, their extensive preoccupation with the concept of *ilm*, led Muslim scholars not just to produce thousands of definitions of knowledge but also numerous divisions and classifications of knowledge.[13] The most famous of these classifications was produced by al-Kindi (801–973), who was himself a librarian, al-Farabi (d.950), Ibn Sina (980–1037), al–Ghazzali (1058–1111), al-Razi (864–925) and Ibn Khaldun (1332–1403).

As befits such institutions, the librarians were of an exceptionally high standard. The *Fahirist* mentions three librarians who served at one time or another as the librarian at the *Bait al-Hikma* — all were noted authors and translated works from Greek and Persian. The library at Subur was headed by al-Murtada, a man of learning and considerable influence in scholarly circles. The *Dar al-ilm* in Cairo was headed by judge Abd al-Aziz, who was renowned for his grasp of jurisprudence. The profession commanded high respect and a rather good salary. Throughout the *Fahirist*, al-Nadim shows clear signs of jealousy towards the librarians of the House of Wisdom because of their high standing in society and their scholarship.

Apart from the central libraries, there were also numerous public libraries. In a city like Merv, the traveller and geographer Yakut found no less than twelve. During his three years residence in the city, he gathered the greater part of the material for his geographical dictionary. In the loan of books so much consideration was shown that he kept with him 200 volumes at a time. Baghdad, Damascus, Cairo, Cordova, Fez, Isfahan, Lahore, Delhi, Samarkand, major as well as minor cities, boasted a host of public libraries. Most of these libraries received government subsidies; some were *waqfs* set up by individuals who wished to promote knowledge. The geographer al-Makdisi tells us that during the tenth century, the visitors to the central libraries of Basra and Ramhurmuz received financial assistance to do their work. In addition, the Basra library also had a full-time professor under whom one could study Mutazili thought and ideas.

Apart from public libraries, special libraries for the cultivation of various departments of literature and the sciences were also founded. Hence we find collections of medical books in hospitals; works on mathematics, astronomy and astrology in observatories; religious and legal writings in mosques and colleges; and rich and more diverse collections in several great academies. Thus, almost every social, cultural and scientific institution supported a rich library.

In addition to central, public and special libraries, there were literally thousands of private collections. During the Abbasid period, Yahya ibn Khalid al-Barmaki's private collection in Baghdad was known to be the richest. Each volume in that library had three copies and most of the rare works from *bait al-hikma* were included. During the eleventh century the library of Mahmud al-Dawlah ibn Fatik, a great collector and scribe, became famous because Ibn Fatik spent all his time in his library, reading and writing. His family felt so neglected that when he died they attempted to throw away his books in anger. The library of the noted ninth-century scholar al-Wakidi required 120 camels, with 600 chests, to carry them from Baghdad to beyond the Tigris. Book collectors took pride in establishing libraries and inviting scholars to use them; indeed, it was the main fashion of the time. The historian Makkari relates a story about al-Hadhrami who says:

> I resided once in Cordova for some time, when I used to attend the book-market every day, in hopes of meeting with a certain work which I was anxious to procure. This I had done for a considerable time, when on a certain day, I happen to find the object of my search, a beautiful copy,

elegantly written and illustrated with a very fine commentary. I immediately bid for it, and went on increasing my bid, but, to my great disappointment, I was always outbid by the crier, although the price was far superior than the value of the book. Surprised at this I went to the crier, and asked him to show me the individual who had thus outbid me for the book to a sum far beyond its real value, when he pointed out to me a man of high rank, to whom, on approaching, I said, 'May God exalt you O doctor, if you desire this book I will relinquish it, for through our mutual bidding its price has risen far above its real value.' He replied: 'I am neither learned nor do I know what the contents of the books are, but I have just established a library, and cost what it may, I shall make it one of the most notable things in my town. There is just an empty space there which this book will fill up. As it is beautifully written and tastefully bound I am pleased with it, and I don't care what it costs, for God has given me an immense income.'[14]

Many private collections helped visiting scholars financially and many libraries were made *waqfs* by their owners. Ali bin Yahya al-Munajjim personally received visitors who came to study the books in his library, which he called *Khizanat al-Hikma*, and provided them with food and lodgings. According to al-Makdisi, 'in Dar al–Ilm of Jafar b. Muhammad al-Mausili, the books were made *waqf* for the use of seekers of knowledge; no one was to be prohibited from access to the library "and when a stranger came to it seeking culture, if he happen to be in financial straits, he [Mausili] gave him paper and money". Here the books were made *waqf* for the use of seekers of knowledge without exception, and they were helped financially on an individual ad hoc basis.'[15] It was such devotion to books and libraries that permitted the Muslims, in the words of Ruth Stellhorn Mackensen, to develop 'the library as an institution to unprecedented lengths. Not until recent times have libraries been so numerous, well stocked, and widely patronised as they were in Muslim lands'.[16]

Book Trade and Markets

It is hardly surprising that such intense interest in books generated a thriving book trade. The state encouraged this trade; along with armament and horses which could be used in battle, and ornaments for brides, books were exempt from tax throughout the length and breadth of the Muslim world. Consequently, traffic in books between states was exceeded only by essential goods. Agents of rulers, private collectors, booksellers as well as scholars themselves travelled to different countries, including non-Muslim lands, in search of valuable manuscripts. Adjacent to almost every mosque, was a booth of a small bookseller. But it would be wrong, as Khuda Bukhsh seems to suggest, that all bookshops in the golden period of Islam were small.[17] Indeed, al-Nadim's bookshop, which contained the books described in his massive catalogue, the *Fahirist*, must have been several times bigger than Foyles of London which describes itself as the 'biggest bookshop in the world'. Thus when the historian Yaqubi tells us that there were over a hundred bookshops in Baghdad alone during his time, he is talking about shops of all sizes. Almost all Muslim cities of the classical period had segments of the central bazaar reserved for book traders: *suk al-waraqqan*. The book bazaars of Baghdad, Cairo, Cordova, Saville and Samarkand were particularly famous.

In addition to bookshops, there was another institution in existence during this period which seems to have been overlooked by Muslim historians. This is the institution of *ijarah*. As a legal term, *ijarah* signifies permission granted for a dispensation to use something owned by another person. In the specific context of bookshops, it refers to a book that has been 'hired' not just for study but also for the purpose of, and with the right to copy. Up to the end of the sixteenth century, *ijarah* institutions were a common sight in Muslim urban centres. They were not simply commercial lending libraries but also served as centres for the dissemination of books. When he was young and poor, Ishaq bin Nusayr al-Abbadi went every evening to a certain bookseller in Baghdad and borrowed one book after another for copying. Whenever the bookseller asked him to pay the hire fee that was due to him, Ishaq would tell him to be patient until he had a lucrative position.[18] We do not know whether Ishaq ever paid the owner of the *ijarah*, but within a few years he had an impressive library of his own.

Despite the magnificent royal libraries, numerous splendidly endowed public and semi-public libraries, *ijarahs*, and a thriving book trade, Muslim scholars' demands and appetite for books could not be satisfied. Al-Biruni took forty years looking for and tracking down a copy of Mani's *Sifr al-asrar*. Ibn Rushd wanted to consult certain Mutazilah works to solve some philosophical problems but failed to find them. According to a story by at-Tawhidi, Abu Bakr al-Ihsid had been looking for a copy of al-Jahiz's *Kitab farq bayn an-nabiy wa-l-mutanabbi* yet despite years of search was unable to secure it. So he went to perform the pilgrimage and during his stay in Makkah hired a public crier who called out for a copy at Arafat. Even though the congregation at Arafat was the largest gathering of Muslims from all over the world, Abu Bakr did not succeed in finding the book he desired.

Our brief analysis of the history of Muslim librarianship and book trade shows us how naturally the infrastructure for dissemination of information evolved in Muslim civilization during the classical period. In one respect, it is quite astonishing that in less than a hundred years after the hijra of the Prophet from Makkah to Medinah, the book had established itself as an easily accessible and basic tool for the dissemination of knowledge and information. However, when viewed from the perspectives of such notions as *ilm*, *waqf* and *ibadah*, which the early Muslims incorporated into their lives at all levels, the phenomenal spread of books and bookmen in early Islam does not look all that astonishing. Indeed, when actualized at all levels of society, the conceptual matrix of Islam would work to produce an infrastructure for the dissemination of information in any society even if it had serious flaws. The eternal concepts of Islam are for the real world, they do not operate or have much significance for an idealized society. During the early days of Islam, the dictates of distributive *ilm* and *waqf* were institutionalized in a society that had many serious problems, including, sectarianism — numerous sects were constantly at war with each other and indeed many libraries were established to promote certain sectarian views — disunity and political divisions. But inspite of all this strife, the conceptual matrix produced an information infrastructure that took the Muslim civilization to its zenith.

The contemporary Muslim *ummah* appears to be facing problems even more formidable than those of the early Muslims, including dependency, parochialism, fatalism and economic and environmental disaster. In these circumstances the implementation of the eternal concepts of Islam becomes even more significant. It was the institutionalization of Islamic concepts that saved the Muslims of the classical period from their follies and quarrels. And because they have eternal and universal validity, it is the actualization of these very concepts that can save the contemporary *ummah* from the obvious disasters that loom ahead. Only by rooting their information policy firmly in the matrix of Islamic concepts can Muslim countries generate the type of intellectual energy and productivity needed to meet the problems of the contemporary *ummah*. Evolving strategies based on such notions as *tawheed, adl, ilm, khalifa, ummah, hikma, waqf, istislah*, to meet the challenge of the information age, to utilize the new information technology based on computers and satellites to promote health and harmony in society, is tantamount to reaching forward for the Islamic heritage.

Notes

1. Cited by Ruth Stellhorn Mackensen, 'Arabic Books and Libraries in the Umaiyad Period', *American Journal of Semitic Languages and Literature,* **52** 245–53 (1935–36).
2. *ibid.,* **54** 41–61 (1937).
3. Ruth Stellhorn Mackensen, note 1, p. 252.
4. Edited by De Jong, p. 126.
5. Edited by De Jong, p. 360.
6. For a detailed look at the Muslim art of bookbinding see Gulnar Bosch, John Carswell and Guy Petheridge, *Islamic Bookbinds and Bookmaking,* The Oriental Institute Museum, The University of Chicago, 1981.
7. For a detailed look at the Muslim art of illumination, see Martin Lings, *Qur'anic Art of Calligraphy and Illumination,* World of Islam Festival Trust, London, 1976.
8. F. Rosenthal, *Technique and Approach of Muslim Scholarship,* Pontificium Institutum Biblicum, Rome, 1947, p. 8–9.
9. George Makdisi, *The Rise of Colleges: Institutions of Learning in Islam and the West,* Edinburgh University Press, 1981, p. 24–5.
10. Translated by Bayard Dodge, Colombia University Press, New York, 1970 (2 vols.).
11. Khuda Bukhsh, 'The Islamic Libraries', *The Nineteenth Century,* **52** 125–39 (1902).
12. Islamic Foundation of Bangladesh, Dakkah, 1983, p. 71.
13. See F. Rosenthal, *Knowledge Triumphant,* Brill, Leiden, 1970.
14. This anecdote has been related by numerous historians of Muslim libraries, including Khuda Bukhash, Ruth Stellhorn Mackensen and Shaikh Inayatullah, 'Bibliophilism in Mediaeval Islam', Islamic Culture, **12** (2) 154–69 (1938).
15. George Makdisi, *op cit.,* p. 26.
16. 'Background to the history of Moslem Libraries', *American Journal of Semitic Languages and Literatures,* **51** 114–25 (1935).
17. *Islamic Studies,* Lahore, Sind Sagar Academy, undated reprint of 1926, p. 108.
18. F. Rosenthal, *op cit.* p. 8.

3

Computers and Satellites
A Balanced Approach to the Information Age

The epithet most often used to describe contemporary western civilization and its component societies is 'technological'. The period since the Second World War is usually described as 'the age of technology'. The very fact that our historical epoch is identified with technology means that it is recognized to be one of the main, if not the main, agents of change. Most of the social, economic and cultural changes introduced in contemporary society have been generated by technology with computers and telecommunications in the vanguard.

It was Norbert Wiener who, in his influential *The Human Use of Human Beings: Cybernetics and Society*, first announced the revolution being introduced by computers and other technologies of communication and control in the early fifties[1]. The origins of this revolution have been traced back to 1956 by Daniel Bell[2]: it was the year when the number of white-collar workers in the United States passed that of blue-collar workers. The new revolution was to liberate men from the drudgery of work, shift the economic base from manufacturing to services. Advances in computer and satellite techniques changed the overall focus from technology in general to information in particular. In the early seventies, information science emerged as a new and challenging discipline. By the end of that decade the technological revolution was generally considered to be the information revolution. In his *The Information Machines*,[3] Ben Begdikian described information as the 'soul' of the technological revolution. Before the advent of the computer and other information processing technologies, we were infants; now we are maturing and reaching the apex of our cultural prime.

The Japanese information scientist, Yoneji Masuda, talks of three stages of the information revolution which will have a more decisive impact on human society than the 'power' revolution ushered in by the steam engine. During the first stage of the information revolution, work hitherto done by man is replaced by technology. In the second stage, technology makes possible work which has not yet been achieved by man. In the final stage, the existing social and economic structures are replaced by new social and economic systems. Masuda describes the first stage as automation, the second as problem solving and the third as system innovation. The most serious impact of the first two stages on the third would be the creation of a managed society.

> While liberating us from labor for subsistence and providing us with ample free time, automation will bring the possibility of 'invisible social restraint', so called because it would not entail surveillance by secret police like the GPU but would rather take the form of functional and systemised restrictions through invisible, systems-orientated information. If large-scale data banks should be placed under the control of a handful of rulers for their monopolistic use and for the maintenance of the machinery of power, the potential for social restraint would pose the dreadful danger of a managed society.[4]

Information technology is meant to run all of society on time, not just the trains.

Such rosy representations of information technologies and their beneficial role promotes the notion that computers can do no wrong, they can solve all of society's problems; indeed, they are the magic ingredient which makes information available to all, provide power to poor, marginalized societies to transform themselves into wealthy ones.

Most Muslim countries have been fooled by this idyllic picture of computer and communication technologies. In the mid-seventies, during the euphoria generated by the oil boom, massive computer systems were installed in oil-rich Muslim states. In the Shah's Iran, an imaginary demand for massive, sophisticated computer systems was created. There was to be a computer terminal in every village, a network linked to a central mainframe was to cover the length and breadth of the country containing data on people's movements and keeping the Shah informed of the state of his people. Most of the major Iranian governmental institutions, such as the Plan and Budget Organization and the Social Security Organization installed massive systems far beyond their needs, and handling ability. Moreover, none of these systems actually worked; indeed, the failure and collapse of the systems was so common and so pervasive that the Shah's regime was forced to take the multinational responsible for setting up the system to court.[5]

But the installation of the massive computer network in Iran served one main purpose for the Shah. He was able to use computer technology for repressive ends: for surveillance, holding massive files on the key personnel of the opposition and as a basic tool of the intelligence work of SAVAK, the secret police. Indeed, the main role of information technology so far in the Third World has been for military and repressive purposes. For example, in Argentina under the generals, police and secret service personnel drove cars fitted with highly advanced computers linked to data banks as sophisticated as those in Europe. In Chile, Brazil, Iraq and Syria imported computers have been used largely for repressive ends. No doubt, for Third World despots and dictators it is this aspect of information technology which is most attractive.

But even if they were used for beneficial purposes, and they brought the benefits claimed, would it be possible for Muslim countries to transfer information technology with ease and efficiency? The history of development provides incontrovertible evidence of the absolute failure of transfer of technology projects. The problems faced by developing countries in the adaptation and local use of other types of technology will produce the same hurdles as the Iran experience demonstrates. Eres has summarized the main factors inhibiting the transfer of information technologies to the Third World (Table 3.1).[6]

But suppose these common, and now well understood, problems could be overcome, what immediate advantage would information technology bring to the Muslim world? Undoubtedly the most cited example concerns access to the vast data bases of the industrialized countries. However, considering that information available on the data bases in the North is of no real relevance to the Muslim countries, access or non-access to these data bases is largely an academic point of no pragmatic significance. (This point is argued further in chapter 7.) Consider the example of medicine. In most Muslim countries — Bangladesh, Egypt and Morocco are good examples — hospitals are short of cotton wool, surgical spirits and bandages, malnutrition and lack of hygiene are major killers, diseases such as diarrhoea and bilharzia are endemic; the very notion of applying information technology to medical services is unadulterated madness. What possible gains could, for example, Pakistani medical professionals secure by having access to the American Medlars system, when their main concern is preserving and accumulating information on Pakistan aetiology?

Table 3.1 Factors inhibiting information technology transfer

General factors	Conditions in developing countries
1. Economic	Labour intensive society Low availability of capital Inability to absorb recurring costs Expense of international activities Lack of internal competition Problems with foreign exchange regulations
2. Manpower	Shortage of available trained manpower Low prestige of information professionals Difficulty in recruiting specialists Lack of continuing education
3. Physio-ecological	Limited resources Geographic isolation
4. Cultural, demographic, and social	Many unskilled workers Language barriers Inaccurate expectations of technology Information-seeking behaviour of scientists and technicians, especially its low priority
5. Political	Unstable governments Desire for often excessively tight security and secrecy Constantly changing priorities Centralization of decision-makers Lack of scientific impact at highest levels of government
6. Existing information infrastructure	Inadequate and unreliable telephone, postal and electricity supply services Tight, stringent customs systems Inability to join telecommunications networks Lack of library and information standards Insufficient hard-copy collections Absence of sufficient informal information flow

Apart from the almost complete irrelevance of western data bases to Muslim countries, the flow of data between national boundaries also has some undesirable side-effects. These were articulated by Canada in 1979 when it produced a list of reasons to justify its policy of regulating transborder data flow. The list stated that the control by foreign companies over the production and processing of data ran the risks of:

1. Decreasing national control over the interruption of services resulting from technical breakdown or work stoppage.

2. Decreasing the national restraints in producing technology that might violate privacy.
3. Increasing dependence on foreign experts which, at the same time, reduced the possibilities of developing human and technical resources administered in the national interest.
4. Preventing the exercise of local jurisdiction over foreign companies which operate nationally and which store and process their data outside local boundaries.
5. Undermining the national telecommunications system through the use of direct transmission satellites.
6. Allowing the publication of confidential information.
7. Giving a particularly important role to foreign data banks as well as to foreign values, products and services.[7]

That such effects of transnational data flow would lead to loss of national identity is now beginning to be recognized in technologically more advanced developing countries, such as Brazil and India. Both have disclosed similar sets of anxieties to justify protectionist measures against multinational information technology companies.

Social Consequences of One-Dimensional Logic

The proponents of the information revolution tend to emphasize it as a product revolution: computers, robots, satellites, fax machines, electronic mail, videotext, electronic funds transfer, cable, video-phones, computer conferencing and so on — products that we are urged to consume to improve our lot. What is largely overlooked is that the information revolution is as much a process revolution as a product revolution. It is having a profound effect on the process of living, on conventional production, as well as on the process of thinking itself.

It is on thinking that the information revolution is making the most subtle impact. Computers cannot run on information coded in the binary digits — noughts and crosses — but require information to be presented in a highly structured way. To structure information by the use of a computer language and algorithm forces it into a sequential framework: the computer operation is thus given a linear order leading to the chosen solution of the problem under consideration. The very process of using computers to solve a problem first confines thinking to particular, linear and limited domains and secondly entails automatic responses which make thinking superfluous. Four factors enhance this process:

1. The computer languages themselves have only a limited area of applicability. They are closed and their application cannot be extended beyond strict boundaries.
2. In the language of information technology, there is only one word for each meaning and only one meaning for each word. Computer languages operate by means of strict code, eliminating allusion, association of ideas, contradiction, conflict and subjectivity. Information, as we saw in the last section, is an amalgamation of a number of components. The information generated by a computer programme does not reflect the complex, multi-dimensional nature of reality; rather it is a purely linear and artificial creation.
3. The algorithm retains only one solution even though there may be many others; but the logically linear nature of the algorithms excludes them by definition. Moreover, the solution has to be capable of translation into the computer language currently employed; this language therefore influences the choice of solution.
4. If a finished commercial package is being used to solve a problem, the problem has to be rephrased in terms of the package. That is, reality has to be moulded to fit the language of the package.

Thus the computer reduces the process of thought to linear and fixed boundaries and does not permit thinking on different levels or outside the area dictated by its logic and language. And because the computer can manipulate information and solve complex mathematical calculations thousands of times faster than man, we are fooled into believing that the problem has also been solved, that the right and only possible answer has been discovered.

The inherent limitations in computer logic can have a quite devastating impact on society. The larger the computer system, the more powerful its operation, the more prone it is to failure. It is not humanly possible for computer programmes running to millions of lines to be foolproof. The basis of an 'intelligent' computer programme is the 'sequence-response' logic: if this, then do that; it essentially produces hypotheses, or models, of possible future events. It is clearly physically impossible for programmes to cover all possible contingencies. We know how a computer will behave when a programmed event occurs; we have no idea of its behaviour when it meets an unplanned event — aberrant occurrences which were not envisaged in the construction of the programme. Of this aspect of computer behaviour we are simply ignorant. Moreover, this ignorance cannot be overcome: it is implicit in the logic of computers and hence ineradicable. Thus we will always be ignorant of the behaviour of large computer systems controlling nuclear power plants, weapon systems and other complex installations, even though their behaviour could have serious implications for mankind.

The impact of information technologies on the process of production can be just as serious. Massive automation would lead to large-scale unemployment. One computer may make thousands of people redundant. Automation raises other moral dilemmas. In the words of Gurth Higgin:

> If our wonderful new machines take over most of society's work, how are those for whom employment will not be possible, first, to have an income above a minimum dole and, secondly, how are they to fill their time and define themselves socially other than as scroungers and layabouts? This leaves us with a value dilemma. On the one hand why should such people have a decent income if they are not contributing to society's work; and on the other hand, there is the ethical problem that if society cannot find that would qualify people for an income, are they to be blamed and punished? Further, if what could be a majority of the population do not have a significant spending power, who is going to absorb the things made by the machines and their attendant elite?[8]

For labour-intensive economies these questions take on an even more urgent, not to say frightening, importance. The only advantage that many Muslim countries have over industrialized states is cheap and abundant labour: the chip, being even cheaper and much more productive, now threatens this economic edge. As computers and micro-robotic systems dominate the mode of production, human labour will become redundant. Up to now Marx's theory of value has held adequately: the increase in value achieved by labour power has resided solely in the control of the mode of production; while the machine has supplied brute power and performed repetitive tasks, humans have been essential for control and management of machines. When these tasks are taken over by computers, labour power becomes superfluous; and Marx's powerful analysis becomes obsolete. The social and cultural consequences of displacing humans from productive forces cannot really be imagined.

Permitting computers to control and manage the productive process can also have serious consequences for the production of knowledge. This lies in the sphere of expert systems: that is, 'intelligent' systems with expert knowledge and the flexibility to learn from 'experience'. Such systems are already making an appearance in areas such as medicine, agriculture and a number of fields of engineering and technology. However, far from increasing our knowledge, they have the potential of actually restricting it.

Jerome Ravetz argues the point as follows:

> Let us suppose that in some crucial sphere of intellectual practice, there is developed a genuinely effective 'expert system', based on the accumulated wisdom of masters in the field, which really performs better than the great majority of practitioners. The system I have in mind need not be rigid and incapable of 'learning'; failures and new ideas can be fed into it, so that *in itself* it keeps up to date with practice. I argue that, the more truly 'expert' and intellectually dextrous the system, the greater are its destructive consequences for human skills and knowledge in the long run. For, the more effective the system, the more surely it will come to monopolize all the craft skills of the practice which had hitherto been diffused among a mass of practitioners, whose shared experience and ongoing debate, from a *broad and diverse base* of experiences and perspectives, keeps knowledge evolving and alive. One might imagine that such problems will be anticipated; and that there will be a 'parallel expertise' of humans, operating in dialogue with the system, kept in being somehow. But how? If the system comes to define good practice, who will defy it, particularly when an error in such a situation could be taken as malpractice, and render the practitioner culpable? So the evolution of knowledge and skills will, in virtue of the operation of the system in a social context of legally accountable human expertise, be strictly limited to what the system itself can encompass.
>
> One can imagine that under such circumstances the system will gradually but inexorably drift out of touch with the inevitably changing realities of the tasks of the professional practice. But how could this drift be detected? Again, paradoxically, the more sophisticated and flexible the system, the more opaque will be its reasonings to merely human analysts and critics. The detection of 'errors' even in straightforward computer programmes is a lengthy, arduous and uncertain operation. How much more so would it be in this case, when the programmes are more complex, the necessary skills among the human are becoming obsolete and eroded? The system will have effectively defined and constituted the only available practice . . .[9]

Thus by its very logic, information technology tends to create systems which become autonomous and totalitarian. Whether they are designed to replace the productive process or human knowledge, speed up communication or generate consumer products, the tendency of information technologies is to create a world based on linear logic, where only behaviour dictated by that logic and approved by the information system is considered of value. In a perfectly ordered, deterministic world, where everything follows a given, narrowly-defined pattern and is completely predictable, meaning and purpose become irrelevant and thought becomes meaningless. Parvez Manzoor's warning, in this regard, is worth noting:

> The Brave New World of AI (artificial intelligence) is ruled by the demi-god of automation. Man need not do what may be accomplished by the machines,

seems to be inscribed in its holy creed. In this narcissistic universe of self-gratification, there is no room for self-sacrifice. Little wonder that the instrumentalist approach to thinking and the computational approach to intelligence have today triumphed over the human-centred ideals of self-transcendence. Today, the technical mind is making its impudent assault on the last bastion of human autonomy — the human mind. If man earlier could take comfort in his being free in mind and thought, he has reasons to be apprehensive today. What AI aims at is not the *simulation* but the *replacement* of human thought.[10]

Such dire warnings indicate that information technology represents a formidable challenge to the preservation of Muslim identity and culture as well as its autonomy and independence. Even a micro-computer parachuted into a remote, deprived area of the Muslim world needs to tap the whole macrostructure of its place of production to function properly. It thus produces a 'radioactive' microcosm of the ideology and the society of its origin; a single micro-computer has the potential of total cultural subversion. As such, what is at stake for the Muslim people is a complete restructuring of their world according to the ideology of those who manage and control information technologies. Muslim countries therefore need to take a very critical look at information technologies and assess their potential, as well as their hazards. While it is clearly not possible to ignore computers and other information technologies, we must be aware of the dangers they represent and critically evaluate the specific role they can play in improving the condition of Muslim people and reconstructing Muslim civilization.

Information Technology and the Ethics of Islam

It is the deterministic aspects of a society controlled by computers which contains the greatest risks for the Muslim world for it violates the cardinal concept of Islam: *tawheed*. In such a society, there is no place for an omnipotent God because every thing can be determined, predicted and is perfect by definition. Moreover, such a society would eradicate diversity of cultures and not recognize, or indeed permit, non-linear modes of thought and actions. Because they offer a form of apparently total control, computers can come to acquire an omnipotent role in society. It is not by chance that much of modern science fiction casts the computer in this role. Contrast the Newspeak of Orwell's *1984* with the jargon of information technology. Or how in a short story, '*The Machine Stops*', E.M. Forster sees the role of a computer-like machine in the guise painted by the more enthusiastic proponents of computer communication. Written twenty years before the emergence of commercial television, Forster's story shows the inhabitants of the world living in private cells where all interpersonal contact is made through the ubiquitous and godlike Machine. Emotions, curiosity, passion, and adventure are unknown; people either communicate clinical information to others or listen to their lectures on subjects which have been stripped of direct experience and human dimensions. When the Machine goes wrong and stops, humanity's collective breath immediately expires. Such stories may represent extreme views, but even a casual comparison of Forster's people with a whole generation of computer freaks and 'hackers' who know nothing but the computer and are obsessed by it, imparts an uncanny truth to his story. Computers contain the real possibility of becoming godlike and thus violating the notion of *tawheed*. Who needs God, when computers with superbrains and super-processing power become the sustainers and nourishers of society?

Computerized systems also violate other values of the conceptual matrix of Islam. They undermine the notion of *khalifa*: when all aspects of society are handled by computers man becomes redundant and his trusteeship becomes a mirage. As he neither controls nor manages, his role as the representative of God becomes meaningless. The replacement of people with computers violates the notion of *adl*. It is unjust for a state not to provide opportunities for work for its citizens; and deliberately to deny its people, by promoting computer-orientated rather than labour-intensive production, opportunities to earn enough to meet their own and their family's basic needs is the height of *zulm* (injustice). As tools for political repression, information technologies clearly go against the dictates of *adl*. Moreover, the tendency of computerized systems to lean towards, in the words of Yoneji Masuda, 'invisible social restraint', means that they will intrinsically violate the dictates of *istislah*. Public interest is not served by permitting those with access to large data bases to manipulate the citizens socially and economically. Neither is public interest promoted by the invasion of privacy associated with gathering large amounts of data on the personal affairs of the citizens. When the process of acquiring knowledge is reduced to the clinical manipulation of information, *ilm* ceases to become a virtue. Now, it is not so much an *ibadah*, a form of worship, it is more a mechanical exercise. And by submitting to the limitations and constraints that a computer design imposes, the 'tyranny of code', other ways of thinking and solving problems are ignored. Linear clarity is achieved by limiting what can be expressed and transmitted. The most important aspect of information, its ability to surprise, disappears. There are people who are never amazed by anything and never learn anything new because they have crude ideas in all matters and fixed views on all things. Computerized information is like them: it hides the complexities of reality by reducing it to logical categories. Hiding from complexities and relying on simple notions and linear solutions is not a sign of *hikma*. Open mindedness, shrewdness and the ability to grasp the complex interconnections of the process of living is something that computerized systems do not promote. They thus also violate the Islamic notion of *hikma*.

Working Towards Positive Ends

As computerized systems undermine so many of the cherished values of Islam, their wholesale incorporation in Muslim societies is not a good idea. In particular large computerized systems which try to link the entire apparatus of the state, such as those established in Iran under the Shah, should be positively avoided. Industrial automation should also be shunned where it creates unemployment by replacing human labour with computers. The development of large data banks of personal and financial information on the citizens, and information systems which increase government potential for invasion of privacy through the connection of various data banks, must also be checked. In general, it is the aspects of information technologies which tend to control, manage and manipulate thought and action — at present the dominant aspect — that needs to be avoided in Muslim societies.

An awareness of the dangers inherent in information technologies for Muslim societies is the first step towards checking their destructive use. However, information technologies also have the potential for solving many problems in Muslim societies.

It is in the use of information technologies as *distributive and decentralized networks* that their greatest potential lies for Muslim societies. While large information systems are designed to control and manage, and tend to be compulsory and totalitarian, microcomputers have the ability to help poor societies grapple with their equity problems and develop autonomous and independent cottage industries. Moreover, certain information technologies can be used to unite and integrate the Muslim world. For example, cheap microcomputers can be used to *supplement* literacy programmes: microcomputers can create conditions for people to learn to read and write with greater ease and lower costs. Rural communities can use microcomputers in conjunction with telephones for access to medical, agricultural and other relevant or vital information. Remote communities can use VHF or UHF radios, operating on batteries and equipped with telephone dialling facilities, to communicate with each other and with regional information centres.

While the microchip creates unemployment, it also presents an opportunity for entrepreneurs with limited capital to develop small industries. Up to now, cheap labour has been used to provide competitive advantage for developing countries in the international markets. The much-quoted South Korean/Taiwanese model of industrialization through manufactured exports is based on exploitation of abundant low–wage labour, long working hours and ruthless suppression of industrial action. However, this model is based on centralized use of computer technology and follows the established western pattern of 'development' through imported technology and export of finished consumer products (largely) to industrialized countries. Moreover, this conventional approach to industrialization meets conventional resistance: import restrictions and protectionism. For example, South Korea's colour television industry has not been granted PAL licences and has therefore been excluded from European markets. Three Korean firms invested $175 million in an effort to promote exports to the US but were unable to break through the import control barriers. Thus apart from being based on exploitation and tyranny, this strategy is certain to meet serious resistance and thus has a high probability of failure.

However, if micro-electronics were used not for centralized big industry, but for distributive small cottage industries which were geared towards producing basic goods for markets in the Muslim countries, the situation would be entirely different. Micro-electronic systems have been largely used in consumer products like televisions, video-recorders, hi-fi, compact disc players, washing machines and microwave cookers. But suppose they were used in products that were acutely needed in Muslim societies: simple power tools, sack makers, tools and instruments for production processes such as the manufacture of glass, soap and light bulbs. Electro-mechanical technologies being used for producing basic need products in Muslim societies are cumbersome, unreliable and expensive. As micro-electronic circuits do not have moving parts they reduce the need for repair and maintenance, are generally more reliable, cheaper, easier to use and offer a greater range of functions. Moreover, the skills required for designing and setting up micro-electronic systems are rudimentary in nature — graduates from local technical colleges could easily be trained to have both the necessary knowledge for designing and implementing such systems. As the products of this process are geared to meeting local and regional needs, they would make a positive contribution and find a ready market. Malaysia,

Pakistan, Turkey and Egypt have all the manpower and technical base to introduce this type of distributive use of computer technologies.

Let me give two further examples of the positive impact of information technologies. First is indigenous telemedicine which uses telecommunications technologies to assist in delivery of health-care. In areas with inadequate health-care facilities and lack of medical manpower, a system which converts telephone transmitted audio signals into black and white television pictures can be used to assist on-the-spot diagnosis and treatment by consultants who do not have the time and resources to attend to patients in remote areas. Pictures of X-rays, EKGs, skin lesions, pages of text and charts can be sent and stored on discs or tapes.[11]

The second example concerns the telephone — one of the most versatile and useful products of the information age. Telephone systems in the Muslim world are most inadequate and inefficient. It is quicker to ring from Dakkah to London then it is to phone any other major city in Bangladesh. In Karachi you have to wait hours to get a line and you are restricted to three minutes: the operator cuts you off mid-sentence. In Cairo it can take hours, sometimes even days, to place a call. Even if one is lucky enough to find a working telephone and get a line, half the time one has to put up with crossed-lines and the other half with unnecessary noise which makes it impossible to hear the other party. It is estimated that in an average Third World city, 40 man-years of time are wasted every day by people dialling useless telephone calls. Yet telephones are vital for the survival of any nation in the information age. They are *the* key for economic development and national integration. Moreover, telephones promote the Islamic notion of *shura* as people can consult easily and openly with each other on the phone; and once open consultation becomes the norm, *ijma*, or consensus of views, follows. Moreover, wide use of telephones tends to reduce the abuse of power. It has been estimated that the critical point at which a country's autocracy or bureaucracy finds it has to restrain its power is when 20 per cent of the population have telephones. Person to person telephoning across the mass of the population promotes consensus and free exchange of information which acts as a catalyst to healthy development.

It is not much use suggesting that telephone systems should be improved, for designing and installing a modern telephone system is a very costly affair; and most Muslim countries cannot meet this cost. An idea of the costs involved can be appreciated from the fact that Saudi Arabia's telephone system, installed by Bell Canada, carried a $5 billion price tag.

However, information technologies offer a much cheaper solution.

Most of the Muslim world can be connected by telephone within ten years by satellite technology. Muslim countries have to pool their resources to put up one or two strategically placed satellites which would link almost every village from Morocco to Indonesia.

Even in the positive aspects of information technologies there are traps of which we have to be aware. The first is control. The true benefits of information technologies will accrue to those who control it. Thus there is not much point in having elaborate programmes to set up communication networks to link remote villages if one is dependent on technology from the industrialized countries. As such, even enlightened policies will end up only generating dependency. Secondly, there is the question of inappropriateness. The technologies generated in the West are specifically geared to the use of western consumers. These are important reasons for the Muslim world to develop indigenous capabilities in micro-electronic technologies. Failure to do that means further dependency on the industrialized countries which will lead to their maintaining their economic and political domination in further subverting and subjugating the Muslim world.

Muslim countries do indeed possess the technological ability to develop micro-electronic technologies; it is an enterprise that ought to be undertaken collectively with a number of Muslim countries cooperating to explore and develop particular areas.[12] Certainly there is absolutely no need to import software: Muslim countries have both the technical skills and intellectual power to develop all the software they need. And where it becomes absolutely necessary to import certain kinds of hardware, its change and modification at the point of use should become an article of faith.

The positive potential of information technologies can only be enhanced by critical evaluation and assessment of their use to Muslim societies and culture by judging them against the conceptual values of Islam. As has been the case with other technologies, Muslim decision-makers are in a real danger of being seduced by hardware and software salesmen and 'aid' packages from the industrialized countries. Information technologies will benefit Muslim societies only when their production and control is completely in Muslim hands; and only when they are developed with a critical and balanced approach. Ultimately, it is only by developing appropriate information technologies, geared to meeting their specific needs and value criteria, that Muslim countries can survive with integrity and independence in the information age.

Notes

1. Norbert Wiener, *The Human Use of Human Beings: Cybernetics and Society*, MIT Press, Cambridge, Massachusetts, 1948.
2. Daniel Bell, *The Coming of the Post-Industrial Society*, Basic Books, New York, 1973.
3. Ben Begdikian, *The Information Machine*, New York, 1971.
4. Yoneji Masuda, 'Automatic State vs. Computopia: Unavoidable Alternatives for the Information Era', in: Andrew A. Spekke (ed.) *The Next 25 Years: Crisis and Opportunity*, World Future Society, Washington D.C., 1975. See also his *The Information Society as Post-Industrial Society*, World Future Society, Washington D.C., 1980.
5. Ziauddin Sardar, 'Scientific Thinking behind Khomeini', *Nature*, **282** 439–41 (1979).
6. B.K. Eres, 'Transfer of Information Technology to Less Developed Countries: A Systems Approach', *Journal of the American Society for Information Science*, **32**(3):97–102 (1981).
7. Armand Mattelart, 'Infotech and the Third World', *Radical Science*, **16** 27–35 (1985).
8. Gurth Higgin, 'Information Management: Taking Account of the Human Element', *Aslib Proceedings*, **37** (2) 91–8, (1985).
9. Jerome Ravetz, 'Computers and Ignorance', *Inquiry*, **3**(9) 40–44 (1986).
10. S. Parvez Manzoor, 'The Thinking Artifice: AI and its Discontents', *Inquiry*, **3**(9) 34–9 (1986).
11. These examples are from Frank Feather and Rushmi Mayur, 'Communications for Global Development: Closing the Information Gap' in Howard F. Didsbury, *Communication and the Future: Prospects, Promise and Problems*, World Future Society, Washington D.C., 1982.
12. For a detailed analysis of scientific capabilities of the Muslim world, see Ziauddin Sardar, *Science, Technology and Development in the Middle East: A Guide to Issues, Institutions and Organisation*, Harlow, Longman, 1982; and M. Ali Kettani, *Science and Technology in the Muslim World*, Jeddah, IFSTAD, 1986.

4

Traditional and Modern

The Development Function of Information

The concept of development is directly related to the integrity and survival of the Muslim world in the information age. All Muslim countries seek to 'develop' and be at par with the 'developed' countries of the North. 'Development' is seen as the answer to 'backwardness', technological dependence and the continuation of the legacy of colonialism. Since they acquired their independence in the late forties and early fifties, Muslim countries have been zealously following development strategies designed to transform what are seen as 'medieval' and 'traditional' societies into modern ones.

Until quite recently development was considered to be synonymous with modernization, defined as 'the process by which a society comes to be characterised by a belief in the rational and scientific control of men's physical and social environment and the application of technology to that end.'[1] The basic assumptions of modernization and hence development were those of a linear teleology as accepted by the industrialized nations. When industrialization ushered in certain social and medical problems — violence and alienation, juvenile delinquency, mental illness and so on — aware people were forced to acknowledge that the costs of modernization can be heavy.[2] However, it was not until the emergence of the environmentalists and ecologists that the alleged normative superiority of modernity over traditionality was really challenged. The ecologists marshalled convincing arguments in favour of traditional cultures and pointed to the destructive and disruptive side-effects of modernism. The arguments challenged 'the rational and scientific control of men's physical and social environment and the application of technology to that end'. Both science and technology began to be now forcefully criticized for their adverse effects on society and environment.[3]

With the rise in environmental consciousness, development came to be associated with conservation and environmental concerns. The United Nations Conference on Human Environment (Stockholm, June 1972) was one of the first in a long series of major international exercises which led the way to expanding the concept of development. Furthermore the emergence of OPEC, and of India and Brazil as major technological powers, destroyed the conventional notion of developed and developing countries; it now became necessary to distinguish between capital rich and capital poor developing countries as well as between developed countries and less developed countries.[4] By the end of the decade, the modernist concept of development, introduced by Lerner and Rostow and based on indicators such as urbanization, general consumption, illiteracy rates, and on notions such as 'take off', 'stages of growth', 'trickle down theory' and forced suppression of traditional society, were thoroughly discredited.[5] Development now became associated with a whole range of ideas. The contribution of the Pugwash Conference on Science and World Affairs to the United Nations Conference on Science and Technology for Development (Vienna, August 1979), denounced the conventional notion of development based on the transfer of technology and trickle-down effect and suggested that development should now take into consideration the following concerns:

1. Economic growth does not by itself lead to social development and increased general welfare which involves the satisfaction of basic human needs (adequate food, shelter, health, education and employment, in particular), especially of the lowest social and economic strata of the population.
2. Meaningful development involves participation of the people themselves in the shaping of economic and social change.
3. As development is not a historically linear process, it should not consist simply of a replication in the developing countries of the structures and policies of the developed countries. Many paths to development are possible, including capitalist, socialist and distinctively indigenous 'third ways'. It is important to ensure that the path chosen respects the cultural heritage and social values of the society concerned.

4. Industrialization processes in the developing countries should not merely be a graft of certain industrial activities from the developed countries, whether for exploitation of minerals or for producing wage goods locally or manufacturing for export. Industrialization has to be accompanied by the acquisition of the related technologies.
5. Mere transfer of technology is not enough. Even if technology is freely available, a nation cannot develop unless it has a science and technology infrastructure of manpower, knowledge, skills and innovative and productive capacities to absorb and adapt the imported technology. Developing countries must therefore be self-reliant, both individually and wherever possible collectively, so that their slender science and technology resources may be pooled to maximum effect.
6. One cannot have two types of science, one for the developing countries and the other for the developed countries. Developing countries should not be satisfied with a derived culture in science which is continually dependent on developed countries. For this reason, a national capacity for basic research is as important for developing countries as for developed countries, although the problems dealt with and the criteria of choice will often be different.[6]

Other strategies for development, as well as analysis of the notion itself, have expanded the concept further. The United Nations Conference on New and Renewable Sources of Energy (Nairobi, August 1981) emphasized the use of renewable energy sources — solar, wind, biomass — and meeting the energy needs of the rural communities, particularly the supply of firewood, as essential for any sane strategy for development. The First World Congress on Development organized by the World Social Prospects Study Association (Dakar, January 1981) identified basic needs, rural development and dignity through work and employment as the essential criteria for development. The definitions and strategies for development have now become so diverse and numerous that an OECD study, seeking to redefine development, reached the conclusion that the question 'what is development?' is as difficult to answer as the question 'what is man?'. The study concludes:

A whole constellation of economic, political, social, legal, educational and other practices and ideologies have been deployed around the concept and idea of development. Their manifestation express the undeployed original meaning of the term. Accordingly, any definition of development involves a definition of the problem area in which this enormous question has to be asked. The economic theory adopted, the economic practices applied and the policies pursued, constitute the discourse of development and express its implicit meaning. But in their turn, these historic tasks reflect a representation of the world and of the role of human beings of the world. The meaning of development is defined by the meaning men give to their overall social existence through economics and politics.[7]

In the early eighties, development took yet another turn with the emergence of the notion of interdependence. Leaders from the industrialized countries began to talk increasingly about interdependence of North and South and of the idea that the development of the South was a necessity not just for the survival of the developing countries, but also for the survival of the North. While the ecological notion of interdependence is relatively new, in its economic form interdependence stated an old idea. It was first expressed in the Pearson report *Partners in Development*,[8] which reviewed twenty years of economic development. The two reports from the Brandt Commission, *North–South: A Strategy for Survival* and *Common Cause* updated and revived the concept.[9]

Economically, the North has always been dependent on the South both as a source of raw material and as a market for its technology and consumer goods. However, the notion of interdependence introduces a new dimension: essentially it is an argument for maintaining the *status quo* and undermining the Third World demand for a new economic order. 'We are all in the same boat,' goes the argument, 'if you shake the boat, we will all sink.' Development strategies which emphasize interdependence, therefore seek to maintain the unjust global economic, political and technological superstructures and seek reform within this framework.

Economically and technologically, the world is structured as though the developing countries were the colonies of the industrialized countries. About 90 per cent of the scientists live in developed countries and technology is one of their main exports. Banks and insurance companies, airlines and shipping companies of developed countries all tie the world together. The framework for this economic web was set up at the end of the Second World War, by the Bretton Woods Conference, held in the town of the same name in the USA. It set up the World Bank and the International Monetary Fund. At that time most of the Third World countries were still colonies and their role in the world monetary and technological system reflected their subordinate status. They were not party to the Bretton Wood accords. Foreseeing the loss of their empires, the western nations made institutional arrangements for continuing their domination and exploitation of the newly-emerging nations. There have been some minor modifications since then; but essentially the world's economic system is fundamentally the same and reflects the world of the 1940s and 1950s. The notion of 'development through interdependence' is an argument for preserving this structure. For the Third World economies, interdependence becomes dependence as they are subordinated to the power of those who control the world market, advanced technologies and the means of production.[10]

The impact of the colonial structure of the world is well illustrated in the General Declaration of the Consumer Association of Penang's seminar on 'Third World: Development or Crisis' (Penang, November 1984). Over a hundred thinkers, writers and activists from the Third World described the *development problematique* in the following words:

> Although most of the Third World countries have attained political independence, in many ways we are being subjected to more control by our former colonial masters and the industrialised countries. This is true in the spheres of economics, social issues and culture.
>
> In the economic sphere, Third World countries have become even more dependent on the rich countries in the post-World War Two period. Our Third World countries have been sucked even more into the world market, with more of our resources and labour force being used to produce goods for export to the rich countries. Yet the terms of trade of Third World countries have by and large deteriorated vis-à-vis the industrial countries, thus causing hundreds of billions of dollars of real resources to be transferred from the poor to the rich countries.
>
> In the Third World, the best quality lands are planted with crops for export to the rich countries. The richest of our forest, mineral and metal resources are exported to the rich countries. Our best brains and a very substantial part of our labour force are used in the service of transnational corporations (TNCs) owned by the rich countries. Almost all our traded goods are carried on ships owned by rich countries. The international chain of commodity traders, wholesalers and retailers are controlled by these rich countries. And finally, our top researchers spend long hours conducting research for institutions ultimately controlled by the administration of the rich countries, and large numbers of our academicians, doctors and scientists migrate to the shores of the rich countries in search of greener pastures.[11]

These factors account for the continuing drain of money and resources from the Third World. In the colonial era, wealth from the colonized territories was used in the development of the colonial master countries. This situation has been exacerbated. The so-called 'development aid' of today is only a myth propagated by the industrial North who are, in reality, gaining from the Third World in terms of investment profits, interest on loans, royalties paid for technology, management and consultancy fees, losses due to decline in the terms-of-trade, and taxes lost because of transfer pricing by TNCs. The Declaration continues:

In the social and cultural spheres, the industrial world's control over the Third World can be said to be even greater. The Third World countries have consciously or unconsciously imported models of education, communications, cognitive structures, health care systems, population planning, cooperatives, housing and transportation from the industrial countries. Most of these models are profoundly unsuitable and inappropriate for solving the basic and human needs problems of the majority of the people in the Third World. Instead, these models have mainly benefited a small elite. Thus the 'success' of economic growth in the Third World has very largely flowed to this small minority.

The Consumer Association also agreed that women are among the most exploited people in the Third World for, in addition to economic exploitation, they suffer from social and cultural oppression imposed by men. The position of women in the Third World has not been ameliorated by the development process and in some instances they are worse off as modernization in rural areas has displaced the labour of women.

Even the minds of Third World people are affected by the mass communications and fashion industries of the industrial countries. The Third World is inundated with their television programmes, films, videos, records, books and magazines. This obviously intrudes upon the culture and ways of life of the people. Furthermore, the Consumer Association found, the super–powers often prevented Third World attempts at alleviation:

> And when Third World peoples try to break away from the economic or social chains that bind them to the industrial nations, they are often blocked. For instance, when Bangladesh recently decided to ban hundreds of dangerous or worthless pharmaceutical drugs, the United States government intervened on behalf of the drug industry. And when Third World countries do not follow policies that please the major powers, they can be threatened with invasion, as when the United States invaded Grenada and Russia invaded Afghanistan. Or when international agencies like the UNESCO (United Nations Educational, Scientific and Cultural Organisation) or the ILO (International Labour Organisation) or UNCTAD (United Nations Conference on Trade and Development) endeavour to take up issues on behalf of the Third World, they can be threatened with a pullout of funds, as the United States has done.

Any meaningful strategy for development must seek to break the global structure and provide solutions to these problems. The point here is not just that injustice and exploitation are built in to the System but that injustice and exploitation *are* the System. Developing countries cannot acquire independent status as long as they are part and parcel of the System. Development therefore cannot be based on theories, notions, strategies conceived, devised and designed by external powers; for it to have any significance, both the notion and the strategies for development have to evolve from within the Third World.

Development: A New Paradigm

The knowledge gained from over three decades of debate and discussion as well as practical experience reinforce the conclusions that:

1. The old theories and prescriptions for development doled out by economists, including Third World economists, and implemented by planners have failed miserably and now have no credibility.
2. There are many models of development and the path followed by the industrialized countries is not suitable for the Third World, and that each country should determine its own choice by evolving its own endogenous approach to development.
3. Traditional systems are by no means inferior when compared with modern systems and that it is in their traditions and cultures that the solutions to the problems of developing countries lie.
4. Problems of development are intrinsically interconnected and interlinked and cannot be solved in isolation.
5. The dominant unjust global structures can only be broken if Third World countries increase reliance on themselves and develop cooperative strategies with each other.
6. Internal structures within developing countries are just as exploitative as external global structures and have to be broken if enlightened goals are to be accomplished.

These conclusions have led to the emergence of a new understanding or a new paradigm of development. In the emerging new paradigm, the problems that developing countries are seeking to solve are related to meeting the basic needs of their societies, becoming self-sufficient and self-reliant, ensuring social justice across the whole spectrum of society through community development, and cultural authenticity, that is preserving and promoting their tradition, cultures and values. Table 4.1 summarizes the emerging alternative and identifies some factors that are leading to the paradigm shift.[12]

From the perspective of the Muslim world, the emerging paradigm promotes the basic ethical criteria of Islam. In seeking to bring tradition, culture and values to the centre of debate, it makes them the ultimate

Table 4.1   Emerging alternatives to the dominant development
paradigms

Main Elements of the Dominant Paradigm	*Emerging Alternatives*	*Possible Factors leading to the Emerging Paradigms*
1. Linear economic growth	1. Equal distribution of wealth Social justice Basic needs approach	1. Three decades of experience 2. Publication of the Brandt Reports 3. Failure of the 'trickle down' theory for the distribution of development benefits
2. Transfer of capital-intensive, production-oriented technology	1. Emphasis on labour-intensive, intermediate technology 2. Integration of traditional and modern sectors in a country 3. Concern for the quality of life and the environment 4. Concern for the preservation of cultural authenticity	1. Environmental and energy crisis. 2. Publication of *The Limits to Growth* and other world models
3. Modernization	1. Respect for culture and tradition 2. Cultural authenticity	1. Failure of modernization 2. Cultural awakening
4. Centralized planning	1. Self-reliance and emphasis on self-sufficiency 2. Popular participation in decentralized planning and execution 3. Emphasis on community development	1. Three decades of development experience 2. Cultural awakening in some developing countries
5. Under-development result of internal causes	1. Internal *and* external causes of under-development 2. Inherent bias towards the West in the system	1. Radical criticism of the dominant paradigm 2. The rise of OPEC 3. The emergence of the Group of 77 4. Shifts in world power as illustrated by voting behaviour in UN General Assembly

yardstick of development policies and strategies. Indeed, a community which is self-reliant and self-sufficient in its material and technological needs is in a better position to discharge its responsibility as the *khalifah* or trustee of God for it has more control over its resources and environment. Furthermore, a society that seeks to promote social justice and community development is acting according to the Islamic dictates of *adl* and *istislah*. Indeed, the notion of material and technological self-reliance and self-sufficiency, social justice and community development, and cultural authenticity make development a goal and value-oriented activity devoted to increasing the material, social, moral and spiritual well-being of men and women. This is in fact how Khurshid Ahmad defines the idea of 'development within an Islamic framework'.[13]

In the new paradigm, information acquires fundamental importance. All sectoral activities (agriculture, industry, transportation, national economy, rural regeneration) require accurate and timely information to be self-reliant and self-sufficient. Other activities geared towards attaining self-reliance in science and technology (research and development), education or government (planning and decision-making) cannot be carried out without the availability of relevant information. Moreover, the notions of social justice and community development cannot have real meaning unless there is free flow of relevant information between all segments of society. Thus information is the life-blood of the new notion and goals of development. Later, we shall formulate a specific model defining the role of information in development. But first it is necessary to examine the key notions of the new development paradigm more closely.

The basic determinants of the new notion of development, namely meeting basic needs through self-reliance, self sufficiency, social justice and cultural authenticity are, admittedly, difficult to grasp. Particularly, self–reliance is commonly misunderstood. What does it mean to have a community or a nation decide on its own development, taking into account its own resources, potential, capabilities and means, evolving its own 'model' — that is, a kind of development that best enables a people to realize their full potential? What does this mean in a situation that is characterized by domination and dependence, where self-reliant efforts are thwarted and where decisions are already predetermined either by external powers or by local elites? What does it mean to be self-reliant when solutions are ready made, when technologies around one are speedier, more efficient and reliable in solving problems? When an alienating and costly culture has already become attractive and desirable? What does it mean in a situation when people are so deprived that they can only rely on their common experience of oppression and exploitation?[14]

It is important to realize that when we are talking about self-reliance and self-sufficiency we use these terms not just in the limited sense of one developing country but for the Third World. In other words, two or more developing countries, at the same stage of development can cooperate to fulfil each others' deficiencies and become self-reliant and self-sufficient together. Many developing countries suffer from being so small that it is not viable for them to be self-sufficient without coopera-tion from the neighbouring states. Taken in totality, developing countries in general and Muslim states in particular, have the potential for self-reliance and self-sufficiency.

On the national level, a development strategy based on maximizing self-reliance implies efforts to produce key commodities which the mass of its population needs. For example, it requires a major degree of self-sufficiency in food of which there is a tremendous shortage in the Third World. By the year 2000 the food deficit is expected to be 100 million tonnes. About 100 million children under the age of five are always hungry. Fifteen million children die each year from malnutri-tion. Yet, Third World countries export about 3.5 million tonnes of high-quality protein every year to the industrialized nations; in return they get 2.5 million tonnes of low-quality protein in the form of grain. This absurd system must be restructured for the benefit of the people of the Third World.

Self-reliance also means reducing dependence on external trade, foreign loans and investments, reduction of imports, especially of luxuries, and an end to large-scale transfer of technology. The provision of basic needs for the mass of the people is ultimately linked with any self-reliance policy. This means that local industry must have the cap-ability of producing basic consumption goods.

Self-reliance is intrinsically connected to social justice. Under the political systems which exist in many developing countries, there is little chance of equitable distribution of wealth to enable the poor to attain a minimum standard of living. Self-reliant strategy is meaningless with-out greater participation by the people. Satisfying basic needs requires the participation of the people in locally-based institutions as well as fundamental changes in the distribution of assets such as land and income. This means far-reaching land reforms.

Community participation as a process permits a peoples' development of themselves, their lives, their environment. But the people cannot participate in the development of their community if they do not have some power. Thus in matters such as housing, the poor must be given appropriate authority and opportunity. Self-help and mutual-help housing projects, with land tenure security and adequate capital, are therefore keys to self-reliant development. Health is another example in which the active participation of the rural people themselves achieves the best results. Community participation then, is the process by which individuals, families or communities assume responsibility for their own health and welfare and develop the capacity to contribute to their own and the community's development — it is thus directly concerned with redistribution of power in society.[15]

And finally, to the notion of cultural authenticity. This does not only mean that traditional cultures, environment and values should be respected. It also means that traditional systems should be seen as a source of strength, and solutions to people's problems should be sought within them. Firstly, cultural authenticity requires emphasis on indigenous development stemming from rural cultures, and the protection of traditional cultures from the onslaught of western patterns of consumption and those consumer goods that represent the omnipotence of technology. It requires deep respect for norms, language, beliefs, arts and crafts of a people — the very factors which provide richness and meaning to their lives. Secondly, cultural authenticity means that traditional systems — which have proved to be more ecologically sound and conservation orientated than their modern counterparts — have to be protected and helped. For example, in many developing countries, traditional systems of medicine still exist. Their support and development and combination with modern medicine would improve the health delivery system in the Third World and reduce dependency on pharmaceutical companies. Similarly, traditional housing techniques, fishing methods and indigenous technologies must become basic components of self-reliant development.

These then are some of the basic building blocks for the new understanding of development. Self-reliance, self-sufficiency, social justice and cultural authenticity are not just conceptual constructs, they also have strong, specific policy implications. It is in this framework that information acquires a central role for development.

Information Science and Development: Towards A Model

The relationship between information and development is one of the least explored areas of information science. When the information needs of developing countries are discussed in the literature, they are seen largely in terms of the conventional notion of development with technology transfer as its basic component. For example, Tell describes as a breakthrough, indeed 'a new model', the fact that a developing country 'coordinates all such activities' as carried out by libraries, archives and documentation centres using 'computer and communication technologies' to set up an 'intelligence function' for promoting technology transfer.[16] Woodward thinks that 'development involves the introduction and adaptation of technology and concepts developed elsewhere'.[17] Salem sees information science purely in terms of 'science and technology transfer between developed countries and underdeveloped countries'.[18]

In contrast, in librarianship the role of libraries in developing countries has received relatively more serious attention. This is largely because it can be readily seen that if libraries have a social function, then they may have a particular role to play in developing countries.

Many authors see libraries as social institutions. Landheer, for example, considers libraries to be social institutions which are developed when their institutionalization requires the raising of consciousness from individual to collective level. He cites examples from European history to support this assertion and concludes that this group consciousness is of particular importance in the case of developing countries:

> The library is the outcome of the growth of a collective consciousness which it in turn stimulates. In our present world, this would mean that the library for the native vernacular or the library of a specific cultural group could become a factor of increasing importance. The library could be of significance as a force against the destruction of culture pattern without any adequate replacement. If a group formation is of importance for the formation of libraries, their best possibilities lie in linking themselves to this group consciousness rather than in trying to change it. The group consciousness precedes the library and the library cannot create it.[19]

Thus, for Landheer the library is a passive social institution. It does not induce change, but reacts passively to it. It does not create group consciousness, but merely becomes an instrument of their propagation. It is a tool created by ideology and used to further its own end.

> If the factor of group consciousness is brought into the picture, it becomes clear why the twentieth century brought the 'ideological library'. The twentieth century, because of its rapid social change, needed a re-examination of all social values and the most decisive method to achieve this was to attempt to reconstruct the social group consciousness directly. This led to the efforts to create a communist mentality which was counteracted by the reconstruction

of the western spirit. This, in turn, led to the modernisation of the mentality of the Islam[ic] countries, the 'third way' of India and the ideological patterns which are emerging in other parts of the world. The Communist library has become a standard feature of the Eastern bloc while the West has seen a considerable increase in publications which analyse its cultural patterns. Regional organisations also build libraries which have an ideological flavour though much of their task is technical. The modern government information library also has ideological goals, though again its purpose includes many more technical goals.[20]

But is it reasonable to assume that libraries, and other kinds of information services, are simply passive instruments of ideological propagation? Or can they also acquire more dynamic social and ideological roles? Benge suggests that the very content of libraries, that is the information sources they contain, is ideologically biased. It is not difficult to illustrate, he writes, that

all the major printed reference sources produced in the English language were brought out in response to the needs not just of society generally, but of particular classes or social groups, especially those who were becoming dominant at specific times. *The Oxford English Dictionary* was precisely a reflection of British imperial power, as was the *Dictionary of National Biography*. In *every* case it could be shown that various information sources were created to meet particular social needs.[21]

Having established the connection between imperialism and information sources, Benge goes on to observe that the use of organized information is associated with urban middle classes. While certain communities may need information, this need is not always felt. 'This is a development problem and something which librarians and information officers have to understand, since part of their job is to identify needs and translate them into concious systems.'

Thus Benge places a more dynamic responsibility on the shoulders of librarians and information scientists. The responsibility of identifying needs and translating them into conscious systems, organized or not, is a key element in understanding the role of information in development. By performing this function, librarians and information scientists make their institutions serve as instruments of raising social consciousness and social change, rather than simply reacting to change as Landheer suggests. Thus a positive feedback loop is established between libraries and other information centres and the level of the social consciousness of a society.

In contrast to Landheer and Benge, J.H. Shera in his classic *The Sociological Foundation of Librarianship* considers libraries to be social agencies, as opposed to institutions.[22] The function of librarians is said to be to 'serve as the mediator between men and graphic records; not only books, but sound recordings, pictures, audio-tapes, charts, whatever contributes to the advancement of human knowledge.[23] The social responsibility of the librarian is seen in terms of a triangle, in which one side is books or graphic records, the other side is people, and the base is books and people. The objective of the library is represented by the base-line: to bring people and books together in a fruitful relationship.

Later, relating libraries to culture, Shera returns to the triangle. One side of the triangle now becomes belief:

> This is the total body of theoretical constructs that the society has evolved, derived from its experience, and coalesced to form their philosophic systems or theological systems or whatever relates man to other men and to the totality of his universe in which man finds himself and to which he must develop a satisfactory intellectual and spiritual harmony. Belief, operating through mores, establishes norms of conduct.[24]

The second side of the triangle represents the physical equipment of culture, while the base is social organization or institutions. The entire triangle represents a threefold division of culture (Figure 4.1).

Figure 4.1   Shera's triangle

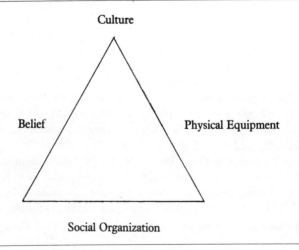

Culture

Belief

Physical Equipment

Social Organization

For the development of a society, all three aspects of culture must develop in harmony. The library is considered to be a social agency as opposed to a social institution and part of the physical equipment of a culture (Figure 4.2).

Figure 4.2   Culture and social organizations

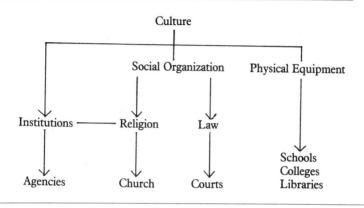

Shera's analysis, although much more thorough, leaves out some crucial aspects of the development function of information science. True, libraries as a part of the cultural equipment of a society, play a vital role in cultural preservation and cultural strength, but what is the role of libraries in social justice, fighting oppression and neo-colonialism, in developing self-sufficiency and self-reliance?

From the perspective of the new paradigm of development, we must seek to understand the role of information in promoting self-reliance and community participation, and social justice and cultural authenticity.

As we discussed above, the notions of self-reliance and community participation have particular policy implications. For example, they require developing countries to abandon the practice of technology transfer; end reliance on imported patented drugs which have been shown to make virtually no contribution to improving the health of Third World nations; and evolve comprehensive strategies for reducing imports, especially of luxuries and dependence on external trade, foreign loans and investment. But in a world structured on colonial patterns, such policies and strategies have met resistance from the industrialized countries. Thus power struggle is an important aspect of self-reliant development. Self-reliance and community participation also focus on traditional modes of doing and being. When communities are allowed to 'do their own thing', it is to the traditional mode of thought and action that they turn. But if customary methods are going to solve modern problems, they must be upgraded. Thus, traditional medicine and methods of building, for example, need to be upgraded and made into a cornerstone for rural and community development. This introduces a value struggle in self-reliant development: conventionally, as we pointed out earlier, modernity has been uncritically considered good and all that is traditional has been looked down upon.

In the pursuit of policies for self-reliance and community participation there are thus strong elements of power and value struggles. The flow of adequate and relevant information is vital for the success of any struggle. If, using Shera's approach, we use a triangle to designate the total area of struggle between self-reliance and community participation on one hand, and dependency — its diametrically opposed concept — on the other, information is represented by the three sides which describe the triangle (Figure 4.3). The goal of information is to steer the power and value struggle away from dependency and towards self-reliance and community participation.

Figure 4.3   Self-reliance and community participation

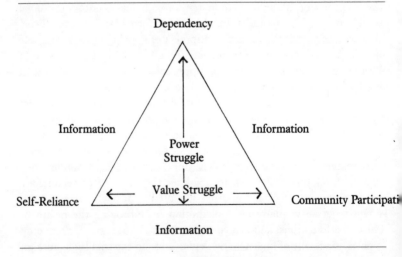

Just as self-reliance and community participation introduce a power and value struggle involving external factors, social justice and cultural authenticity introduce a similar internal struggle. Thus development strategies within the framework of cultural authenticity also take the form of a value struggle: tradition and modernity represent conflicting world views and ideologies and opposing values and norms. Preservation of traditional cultures largely involves preservation of traditional values and norms. What is cultural in a developing society is simultaneously traditional.

Social justice is a *dialectical* concept. It embraces both the macro level of social organization and the micro level of the human mind. Social organization in many developing countries, including Muslim states, is partly a legacy of the colonial past and partly a result of the paternalistic and hierarchical nature of certain traditional societies. Colonialism enhanced the weaknesses and brought the unsavoury features of traditional cultures to the fore, while suppressing their strong and holistic characteristics.

Social justice begins with the rather simple idea that peoples and groups in a developing country should be living for each other rather than against each other and leads to a relatively equal distribution of wealth and social opportunity. Furthermore, it leads or should lead to preservation of what is good and holistic in traditional thought and organization; legal, economic and political arrangements for the equal distribution of wealth and social opportunity; the elimination of distrust between social groups; the promotion of the potential of human qualities; the encouragement of meaningful communication between people, and the elimination of linear-vertical communication and destructive criticism. In as far as social justice demands dissemination of wealth, it concerns itself with politics. And politics, as we all know, is about power.

The reverse of social justice and cultural authenticity is alienation. Alienation, a major characteristic of contemporary Third World societies, arises out of the conflict between tradition and modernity, suppression of traditional culture and thought, acute injustice (social as well as political), illiteracy, political despotism and suppression.

Within the national boundaries of developing countries, basic needs orientated development therefore has two dimensions: it should lead developing societies from alienation to social justice. This is the dimension of power struggle. The second dimension focuses on value struggle: policies that promote cultural authenticity will eliminate alienation. Once again, both these struggles have one catalyst: information. Shera's triangle now takes on new lables: the three sides of the triangle once again describe information whose function is to steer developing societies away from alienation towards social justice and cultural authenticity (Figure 4.4).

Figure 4.4   Culture authenticity and social justice

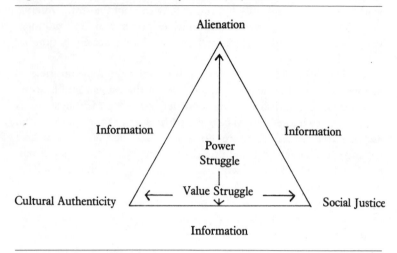

From this model of the role of information in development, we note that information does not follow development but is actually a factor in promoting and initiating it. According to Woodward, four groups of information can be identified in Third World countries:

1. Formal Scientific and Technical Information (STI): information recorded in periodicals, books and major report series and signalled in the major abstracting and indexing services, mostly produced outside the developing countries.
2. Imported information: information brought into a developing country as a by-product of some other activity, e.g. technical cooperation programmes or commercial/industrial activity, largely in the form of acquired expertise.
3. Locally produced information: information generated as a result of research, studies, inventories, development projects undertaken in the country concerned, mostly existing in report form or non-conventional format.
4. Indigenous information: knowledge held by local people, gained and transmitted informally usually by oral tradition.[25]

Thus, at present, much of the information in the Third World comes from external sources: STI and 'imported information' form the bulk of the information available, while locally produced information does not exist in easily accessible forms. Reliance on external sources of information induces dependency and goes against the strategy of self-reliant development. If we ignore the external sources of information, and concentrate on locally produced and indigenous information only, we can synthesize and refine our model: with external elements imposing dependency and alienation removed, the two triangles now become a pyramid. The base of the pyramid is described by self-reliance, community participation, social justice and cultural authenticity, and the area of the base represents the basic needs that have to be fulfilled — it is here that power and value struggles take place in pursuance of a basic needs oriented strategy. Information describes the four sides of the pyramid, while the apex is the goal: development. As we move from the base of the pyramid in pursuit of the goal of development, the power and value struggles become less and less important as more and more basic needs of the society are fulfilled (Figure 4.5).

It is ultimately the internal sources of information, within a developing country and within the Third World, that are intrinsically related to a basic needs orientated model of development. Most industrialized countries possess a whole range of information agencies and services ranging from the national library, and the national documentation centre to specialized information centres, computerized information services and networks, data centres, abstracting and indexing services, public libraries, academic libraries, research and development information units, community information services, commercial information centres, archives, museums, publishers and booksellers. Can we assume that developing countries would also need these services? And should the models that now predominate in the West also be adopted in the Third World?

We have argued that information acts as a catalyst for development and mediates change: it can promote self-reliance and community participation and lead a society towards social justice and cultural authenticity. As social catalysts, information agencies and services do not play an objective disinterested role: their job is to initiate desirable change and help the society adjust to change. They are concerned with both: disseminating information on the individual and societal level, and with the impact of that information on the individual, society and the environment.

As such, information agencies and services in the Third World cannot be uncritically based on western models; neither can we assume that all of the range and services available in the industrialized countries are desirable for Third World countries or indeed would fulfil their needs

Figure 4.5   Development function of information

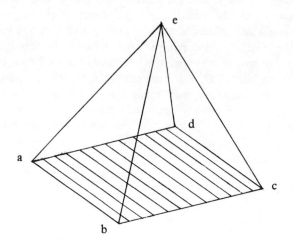

a	Cultural Authenticity
b	Self-Reliance
c	Social Justice
d	Community Participation
e	Development
ac	Value Struggle
bd	Power Struggle
aeb	Information
bec	Information
ced	Information
abcd	Basic Needs

and requirements. While certain kinds of information agencies, such as national and public libraries, are obviously in the Third World, certain others would have to be developed and evolved from their specific needs and circumstances. As Woodward points out, indigenous information exists in non-conventional formats; these formats have to be studied and information agencies geared to the particular shape of this material and the modes of dissemination available in a society have to be evolved. To use the words of Benge, specific needs have to be identified and translated into conscious — not necessarily formal or strictly organized — systems.

Our model of the role of information in development illustrates the fact that information — the four sides of the pyramid — acts as an umbrella for basic needs — the area of the base — orientated strategy for development. The size and nature of this umbrella depends on the extent and variety of basic needs that have to be fulfilled. In other words, the *information structure* of a developing country is a function of its basic needs. Thus a multi-dimensional analysis of the basic needs of a country can provide us with a good indication of the kind of information structure it needs to meet is development goals. On the other hand, an analysis of the existing information structure would indicate the type, quality and quantity of information agencies and the channels of information transfer that exist in a country. It is also a good indicator of the power and value struggles going on within a developing country. The difference between the existing and required information structures should be the predominant focus for information policies in a basic needs orientated strategy for development. We see that the notion of information structure tells us a great deal, both about the level of development of a country and the direction its evolution must take to realize the goals of self-development.

The existing information structures of many developing countries have evolved in rather haphazard ways; they are either a colonial legacy or a result of external pressures. Only a few information agencies in the Third World have grown out of national needs; most are the result of pressure from outside which comes in various forms: 'expert advice', technical aid, salesmanship, tied foreign aid or the more direct forms of brute political blackmail. All these forms of 'aid' direct the evolution of information structures in a particular (dependent) direction, say towards industrialization and production of consumer goods rather than agricultural development and subsistence farming, the resulting technical and economic needs foster certain types of information agencies which produce a rather inappropriate information structure.[26]

A few information agencies have developed out of national needs. Countries with single-crop economies, one-mineral economies and particular health problems have developed specialized information agencies to meet their individual needs. Certain public libraries have evolved to meet the information and entertainment needs of populations. Similarly, national centres for information transfer have been devised to meet the needs of the local scientists and scholars. But the genuinely indigenous information agencies are relatively few.

However, our model of the role of information in development requires the evolution of specific types of information structure interlinked with a strategy for self-reliance and self-development. The nature of the information structure and the types of information agencies that are best suited to this structure would depend on the position of a Third World country on the development continuum. Within this framework, it is not tenable to envisage information agencies in developing countries in general terms. Their functions and development goals have to be clearly defined. Radically different needs, scarce resources, lack of skilled manpower, cultures profoundly different from those of Europe and North America, do not permit the establishment of information agencies based on the ideals of Victorian librarians or zealous information technologists. In most cases, it is necessary to develop new forms of information agencies tailor-made to the needs of Third World societies.

When considering the evolution of appropriate information structures in the Third World, we are also forced to differentiate between information of different kinds. Consider the 'latest' information in a particular technological process for producing glass which is a labour saving, rapid, intensive and highly advanced technological process for the mass production of glass. Now consider another process for the production of glass originating from a place such as the Pakistan Council for Scientific and Industrial Research which is labour intensive, requires a basic level of technology and skill but is low in production. How do we decide which information is more relevant for a particular developing country?

Referring once again to our model: the relevance or irrelevance of information for a developing country is decided by reference to the area mapped out by the basic needs of a country which provides an objective criteria for relevance. It should not be forgotten that this area also describes the cultural, social and physical environment of a Third World country. Thus, the relevance or irrelevance of information is determined not just by basic needs but also by cultural, social and physical determinants. For a developing country, say Malaysia, at a particular stage of the development continuum, where most of the basic needs of the society have been met and a degree of self-reliance and self-sufficiency has been acquired in terms of technology and research base, the information generated in the research establishment of an industrialized country may be more suitable. This, however, would be a rare phenomenon. But for another country, at a different stage of the development continuum, where most of the basic needs have still to be fulfilled and self-reliance is a distant goal, information generated in Pakistan would be more suitable. Given the present state of most developing countries, it can be taken as a general rule that information generated in one developing country is relevant to another developing country. But as individual developing countries move towards the goal of self-reliance, the relevance or irrelevance of particular information has to be established by reference to the extent of their basic needs.

The model of the role of information in development discussed here, as well as the notions of information structure and relevant and irrelevant information, form the basis of much of the analysis in this book. A major hurdle in the basic needs orientated approach to development, the basis of this model, is the image that developing states in general, and Muslim countries in particular, have of themselves and the industrialized countries. To some extent this image is a legacy of colonialism. But this is also a result of what conventional development patterns have done to societies in developing countries. It is to an analysis of the role of information in maintaining this image that we turn next.

Notes

1. John A. Kautsky, *The Political Consequences of Modernization*, New York, Wiley, 1972, p. 20.
2. See, for example, Myron Weinir, *Modernisation: The Dynamic of Growth*, Basic Books, New York, 1966; and M.P. Farvn and J.P. Milton (ed.), *Careless Technology*, The National History Press, New York, 1972.
3. Literature in this field is quite extensive. See Oi Committee International (Compilers), *International Development and the Human Environment: A Bibliography*, Collier Macmillan, London, 1974.
4. For the changes introduced in the world's structure by OPEC, see Ian Seymour, *OPEC: Instrument of Change*, Macmillan, London, 1980.
5. Daniel Lerner, *The Passing of Traditional Society*, New York, 1958; W.W. Rostow, *Stages of Economic Growth*, Cambridge University Press, 1963.
6. Pugwash Conference on Science and World Affairs, 'Pugwash Guidelines for International Scientific Cooperation for Development', London and Geneva, 1979.
7. Alain Birou *et al.*, *Towards A Re-Definition of Development*, Pergamon Press, Oxford, 1977, p. 330.
8. Lester Pearson, *Partners in Development*, Praeger, New York, 1969.

9. Independent Commission on International Development Issues, *North–South: A Programme for Survival*, Pan Books, London, 1980; *Common Crisis, North–South*: Cooperation for World Recovery, Pan Books, London, 1983.

10. For an analysis of how global structure is controlled and maintained see Ziauddin Sardar, 'Last Chance for World Unity', *New Scientist*, **91** 334–41 (1981).

11. Consumer Association of Penang, *Third World: Development or Crisis*, Penang, 1984, p. 9–11.

12. See the excellent work by Peter Oakley and David Marsden, *Approaches to Participation in Rural Development*, International Labour Office, Geneva, 1984.

13. Khurshid Ahmad, 'Economic Development in an Islamic Framework' in *Islamic Perspectives: Studies in Honour of Sayyid Abul Ala Mawdudi*, Khurshid Ahmad and Zafar Ishaq Ansari (eds.), Islamic Foundation, Leicester, 1979, p. 223–40.

14. For an extensive discussion on the subject of self-reliance and self-sufficiency see Johan Galtung *et al.* (eds.), *Self-Reliance: A Strategy for Development*, Bogle-L'Overture, London, 1980.

15. WHO, 'Report on a WHO/UNICEF Intersectoral Workshop on Primary Health Care', Geneva, 1982, annex.

16. B.V. Tell, 'The awakening information needs of the developing countries', *Journal of Information Science*, **1** (5) 285–90 (1980).

17. A.M. Woodward, 'Future information requirements of the third world', *Journal of Information Science*, **1** (5) 259–66 (1980).

18. S. Salem, 'The role of information in science and technology transfer in Arab countries', *Journal of Information Science*, **2** (5) 255–61 (1980).

19. B. Landheer, *Social Function of Libraries*, Scarecrow Press, New York, 1957, p. 212–13.

20. *ibid.*, p. 214.

21. Ronal C. Benge, *Cultural Crisis and Libraries in the Third World*, Clive Bingley, London, 1979, p. 192.

22. J.H. Shera, *The Sociological Foundation of Librarianship*, Asia, Bombay, 1970.

23. *ibid.*, p. 30–31.

24. *ibid.*, p. 55.

25. A.M. Woodward, 'Future information requirements of the Third World,', *Journal of Information Science*, **1** (5) 259–66 (1980).

26. For the havoc such aid programmes and policies have caused in the Muslim World see Ziauddin Sardar, *Science, Technology and Development in the Muslim World*, Croom Helm, London, 1977.

5

Visions and Images
Information and Cultural Subversion

A major factor that promotes conventional, destructive patterns of development in the Muslim world is the image that Muslim societies have of themselves and of western societies. On the one hand, this image acts as a catalyst for blind imitation, inferiority complex and the rush for modernization; on the other hand, it suppresses and thwarts indigenous originality, talent and resources, attempts at self-reliance and self-sufficiency and preservation of tradition and cultural property.

What is this image? Greek mythology provides some parallels which serve as useful analogies. The image most Muslim countries seem to identify with is that of the miserable mother, Niobe, who having lost first her seven sons then her seven daughters was transformed into a rock: *Diriguisse malis* (petrified with her misfortunes). Their image of the occident is that of the all-powerful, all-knowing Greek god, Apollo. Thus, for developing countries, the only way to dignity and identity is to have more of what the West produces, to be nearer to the nation states of the occident, to imitate in every thought, whim and style, to aim for Apollo. This is a new kind of enslavement, one that dehumanizes no less forcefully than physical enslavement.[1]

For its part, the occident uses this cultural power to persuade the Muslim countries to accept its ideas, advice and even its picture of who or what they are. This image, and the mechanism that promotes and nourishes it, has a long history, predating the Crusades; and it has now become an integral part of the mental make-up of western society. It is being perpetuated in a host of disciplines, by numerous scholars and 'experts' on Islam and Muslims, and countless journalists who make a living by writing about Islam and the Muslim world. But before we examine this image in more detail, let us first try and answer the question: what exactly is an image?

An image is a cognitive attribute. It may be a memory or a recollection of a past happening, fact, or opinion. But images are based just as much on belief, tradition, value-systems and culture. They are a product of the social construction of knowledge shaped by our world–view, national character, institutional mould and personal philosophy. This is why we allow images to shape our lives and life–style and much of our environment.

In his classical study *The Image*, Kenneth Boulding indentifies the following as important categories and aspects:

1. The spatial image, the picture of the individual's location in the space around him;
2. The temporal image, his picture of the stream of time and his place in it;
3. The relational image, the picture of the universe around him as a system of regularities;
4. The personal image, the picture of the individual in the midst of the universe around him as a system of regularities;
5. The value image, which consists of an ordering on the scale better or worse of various parts of the whole image;
6. The affectional image, or the emotional image, by which various items in the rest of the image are imbued with feeling or affected by it;
7. A division of the image into conscious, unconscious and subconscious areas;
8. A dimension of certainty or uncertainty, clarity or vagueness;
9. A dimension of reality or unreality, that is an image of the correspondence of the image itself with some, outside, reality.
10. A public/private scale according to whether the image is shared by others or is peculiar to the individual.[2]

This is a particularly western understanding of the image and its role in society. In Muslim societies, and in Third World cultures in general, images do not exist in their varied aspects: spatial image, temporal image, personal image, value image — all are one, reflecting the totality of being of the traditional man. In traditional thought, the image is never cut off from the universe. As the traditional thought of Africa, the South Seas, or Islam demonstrate, man does not set up an angelic image of himself as a singular and in some way ethereal being, confronting the environment, the world, the fauna, the flora, his own body, his consciousness, his sub-consciousness. Here there are no separate dimensions of certainty or uncertainty, clarity or vagueness. The traditional man is an 'anthropocosmos' and nothing cosmic is foreign to him.

In Muslim societies, traditional images condition the operative reality of individuals. Traditional craftsmen, for example, shape a unified reality from their organic image of themselves, their environment, their craftsmanship — all of which are really one and the same image. Introduce an image that does not belong in the total world of the craftsman, say by over-exposing him to consumer advertising, and there will be a conflict between the total traditional image of the craftsman and the modern images presented by the media. The resultant distortion of the traditional mind is quite destructive for the society, the environment and the traditional system itself.

In certain cases the modern images, presented with all the usual force of technology, displace the traditional image of Muslim societies. Various delivery systems advance ten main images, all in direct conflict with the traditional Muslim image, basic needs orientated development strategy, and the priorities and aspirations of Muslim communities. These are adventurism; aggressiveness; conformism; elitism; individualism; materialism; modernism; racism; romanticism; self-defeatism. The power of delivery ensures that the modern images are seen in a favourable light, with the traditional images considered inferior, backward, even savage. An inferiority complex develops: all that is local, indigenous and low-impact is considered inferior, all that is imported, conspicuous and consumer orientated is superior. This distorted image today dominates much of the Muslim world, and indeed the Third World as a whole.

Western Image of Muslim Societies

Fanatics. Incompetent. Fundamentalists. Barbaric. Autocratic. Bloodthirsty. These are some of the terms that have been used to describe Muslims and Muslim societies in the West. The terms, as well as the image they perpetuate, have a long history. In scholarship and literature, as well as in popular fiction and journalism, Muslims are depicted as bloodthirsty savages who chop the hands off thieves, stone non-virtuous women to death, or flog those with a taste for alcohol. The image is perpetuated with such consistency and ferocity that many

Muslims themselves believe in the image and try to live up to the caricature.

There is a very good reason why the Muslims have been singled out as the subject of perpetually distorted images. Islam is the only civilization which has presented in the past, and is likely to present in the future, a serious threat to western intellectual and political domination. Ever since the birth of Islam, and its phenomenal spread, almost in a matter of decades, from Morocco to China, Islam has been seen by the West as the 'other' civilization, the 'other' culture.

Islam has been a lasting trauma for Europe. To medieval Christendom, Islam was problematic. First and foremost, as a problem for Christian theodicy: what purpose did Mohammad serve when God himself had already appeared on this earth? How did the advent of an Arabian Prophet, long after the age of prophecy had culminated in the crucifixion and resurrection of God's son, fit into the divine scheme of salvation? This issue has been nagging at Christianity in its relations with Islam for over 1400 years. But Islam did not present only a religious problem. The might of the Islamic empire was a serious challenge to Christianity. Right up to the eighteenth century, the Ottoman Empire was seen by the Europeans as a constant danger to Christian civilization. The domination of Islamic science and learning for eight centuries clearly demonstrated that it also presented an intellectual problem. And finally, ideologically, Islam was a problem: its hold on the minds of millions of people, even its success in converting millions of Christians, was incomprehensible to Christendom.

To denigrate Islam the West evolved a number of techniques. First, there were straightforward projections of the image with the use of labels. Islam was seen as the dark-side of the European self. So while Europe was civilized, Islam was barbaric. While Europe was peace-loving, Muslims were violent and bloodthirsty. While there was a democratic, freedom-loving tradition in the West, Muslims were despotic and cruel. While Europeans were imbued with morality and virtue, Muslims were amoral, licentious and debauched.

These images have been projected in western paintings and literature since the seventeenth century. European painters like John Leon Jerome, Eugene Delacroix, Horace Vernet, John Federick Lewis and Leopold Karl Müller transferred these images — almost always complete figments of their imagination — to canvas. From Humphrey Prideaux's famous seventeenth-century biography of Mohammad, subtitled *The True Nature of Imposture*, to Dante, Milton, Marlowe, Tasso, Shakespeare, Cervantes, one can find European writers who have peppered their works with these images. For example, in the *Inferno* Dante meets Mohammad in the eighth of the nine circles of Hell. So before he reaches Mohammad, he passes through circles containing people whose sins are less heinous: the lustful, the avaricious, the gluttonous, the heretical, the wrathful, the suicidal and the blasphemous and after Mohammad there are only the falsifiers and the treacherous, before Dante arrives at the bottom of Hell where Satan resides. Mohammad is thus seen to belong to a particularly evil and demonic category. And since he was an imposter and a disseminator of a false revelation, he became, by the natural force of logic, the epitome of lechery, debauchery, sodomy and the entire spectrum of treacheries. And, of course, what is true of Mohammad must also be true of his followers.

European travel writers reinforced this image. Richard Burton, T.E. Lawrence, Freya Stark, Gertrude Bell, St. John Philby, Thomas Arnold — to mention a few — have often mixed their imagination with the reality they saw and experienced to enforce the stereotyped images. Then, of course, there was academia which gave intellectual respectability to the images of Muslims found in European paintings, literature and travel writing. The historically-conditioned vision of Orientalism — the European study of Islam and the Muslim world — was based on two dogmatic assumptions: that occidental civilization was the norm for all human civilization and the Biblical tradition was normative of all monotheism. Orientalism was, and is, very much a colonial enterprise; as a discipline it evolved to justify the position of the colonial masters and exploitation of their subjects as well as to provide insights into further subjugation of the Muslim people. By definition it took Islam to be a 'problem' — a problem to be contained and managed. It is from this Eurocentric perspective of cultural interest that orientalist scholars, such as Schacht, von Grunebaum, Gibb and others, as so ably analysed by Edward Said in his *Orientalism*,[3] have undertaken their studies.

Eurocentricism and the image of Islam as a barbarian culture to be subdued is also central to the thoughts of such European philosophers as Hegel, Marx, Spengler and Toynbee, who have been seminal in the formation of the contemporary western world-view. According to Hegel the historical process had four stages: the Oriental world, the Greek world, the Roman world and the German world which was the apex of the historical process for him. The role of Islam, according to Hegel, was to help bring the fourth world into existence. As Parvez Manzoor points out, for Hegel Islam's emphasis on the worship of One God was

excessive and overwhelming. Islam thus had no interest for the human world and the Muslim mood alternated between pure religious enthusiasm (heroism and also fanatic zeal and ascetic disinterest in the temporal world) and sheer desperation (the love of power and glory). Because of this spiritual ambivalence Islamic civilization was ephemeral and because of its excessive abstractness (it lacked, so he thought, the special attachment which the Jews, for instance, have with the One; or the genuine love for the human which the presence of a *human* saviour bestows upon Christianity) it was also destructive. It was the destiny of Europe, he further prophesied, to absorb the anti-thesis Islam into a new synthesis of its own. Islam now has nothing to offer except 'sensual enjoyment' and 'oriental repose'.

Manzoor's reaction against Hegel is shared by Muslim intellectuals:

One marvels how the most subtle European mind of his time could display such provincial arrogance, such spiritual banality and such intellectual shallowness when it came to Islam! He was a child of his age and his image of Islam was forged in the crucible of western military and political superiority. The Ottoman state was moribund and the rest of Islamic world lay prostrate at the Europeans' feet. It had no effective voice, no philosophy of history, no awareness of its destiny. It did look as if it was destined to perish forever! Hegel was not perceptive or prophetic enough to scan beyond his cultural horizons. The most cogent argument against his indictment of Islam has been provided by the passing of time. The philosopher of history stands refuted by history itself! As for his strictures against the abstractness of Islam, anyone who has the slightest acquaintance with Hegelian thought must spontaneously exclaim: 'the kettle calling the pot black'. To a Muslim who has personally experienced the fullness of his devotion and submission to the One, Hegel also appears ridiculously sham and bogus.[4]

This particular image of Islam and Muslim societies is still very much alive, perpetuated by such recent works of fiction as Leon Uris' *Haj*[5] and Phillip Caputo's *Horn of Africa*,[6] such pretentious scholarship as Daniel Pipes *In the Path of God*[7] and John Laffin's *The Dagger of Islam*[8] as well as in the pages of popular as well as serious newspapers and magazines, in films like *Harem* and *Strike Force* and countless television programmes.

Moreover, it can be found even in modern library literature. Thus, Ronald Benge, otherwise an enlightened writer, cannot help stating that because Islam presents a total way of life this characteristic 'produces doctrinal, practical and political difficulties in relation to the secular aspects of society'. It may indeed produce these difficulties for Benge, but certainly not for the vast majority of Muslims. Benge's description of Islamic education, which has over a thousand years of intellectual history, is a complete caricature based on the reading of a single apologetic and obscure book. When the author, Fafunwa, states that 'traditional education is not any more conservative or any less progressive than any other system',[9] Benge completely fails to understand the significance of the claim or the image the author is trying to fight. Benge then presents the classic orientalist image:

> On a personal level, where individual Muslims have to come to terms with their environment, many adjustments are possible. Islamic truth can be separated from scientific knowledge and the two kinds of symbolic meaning can co-exist, apparently without too much stress. Any integration appears (at least to the outside observer) to be improbable because of the fundamentalist 'revealed' element in Islam.[10]

Thus Muslims, being fundamentalists, can never integrate the modern world with their world-view for 'if the Koran is literally the word of God, then controversy can arise only from its interpretation'! On the following page, Benge sums up the essence of the *Shariah* (Islamic law) by noting that it is in operation in the Gulf States where 'adulterers are stoned, thieves have their hands chopped off, and those who break the Ramadan fast are publically flogged'.[11]

Dominant Image and Cultural Subversion

The dominant image that portrays Islam and Muslim societies as culturally inferior and irrational, and European thought and outlook as modern and progressive has now become integral and intrinsic to Muslim societies. Political leadership in Muslim countries, and indeed in the Third World as a whole, is a legacy of colonialism. It takes its aspiration not from its own culture and world-view, but from Europe. There is thus in much of the developing world a constant tension between the elitist leadership with its occidental world-view and images, and the populace with its, on the whole, traditional outlook and images. It is to the advantage of the political leadership to promote conventional patterns of development and westernized images, to withhold as much information as possible and prevent the development of relevant images in the society. This is one reason why in many developing countries no attention is paid to the development of information agencies and local publication industries, while in some positive steps are taken to check the development of such social and image–forming information agencies. In some developing countries, steps are taken to misinform the populace: considerable strategic gains are made by systematic deception of citizens.

There are three main elements that subvert the formation of relevant images in the Muslim world. First is the political leadership. If, for example, the political leadership considered traditional cities and building techniques inferior and undesirable, it would, on the one hand, encourage the construction of glass and steel sky–scrapers, and on the other hand, allow traditional buildings and cultural property to rot and thus fit the image that had been created for them. Yet, extensive research has shown that the old, tried building techniques as well as cities built according to these methods are best suited to the type of climate, environment and cultural conditions for which they were evolved.

The city, for instance, is a clear expression of man's value-systems, his beliefs and ideals, hopes and aspirations, social outlook and behaviour. As such cities are much more than mere forms, roads and buildings, brick and mortar: they are images of a society's perception of its destiny. The architecture of a particular society evolves with a culture, and the value-system inherent in it.[12] One could introduce a few modern innovations that synthesize harmoniously with the traditional form, but those innovations that generate conflict with the traditional form must be avoided. Architecture in cities like Fez, Sanna and Jeddah evolved around a value-system, lifestyle, local environment and climate. As such it performed a cohesive function in keeping society together, socially and environmentally. When innovation that eventually leads to change in the form, style and content of the architecture is introduced in such cities, they drastically upset the ecology of the city: changes in the built environment also affect values and social behaviour.

For example, the old city of Jeddah with its distinctive character always impressed visitors who passed through its gates. It consisted of a network of remarkable tall houses that made ingenious use of the local meteorological conditions: the uppermost floors were designed to catch the sea breeze which created upward draughts with regular temperature differentials; the overbending, open louvred windows filtered out the sun's glare but allowed air to circulate freely in the rooms; the surrounding flat terraces with wooden grilles permitted the circulation of any cool air currents on the hottest of summer nights. These old houses showed what the power of imagination and craftsmanship of builders could achieve. Exquisite, heavily carved doors with rich, intricate designs and enchanting bay windows adorned most of the houses. When people walked in the narrow streets and alleys they were protected from the sun and cooled by trapped air. When innovation came to Jeddah, wide sun-baked roads and essays in perpendicular, concrete, over-heated monstrosities predominated. Every building in Jeddah is a deadly heat trap and depends on air conditioning to function.

The second element which subverts traditional images and prevents the formation of relevant ones is the educational system. This too is largely a colonial legacy. The image projected by the education system in developing countries reflects an interplay between the value systems of teachers and students, textbooks and syllabuses which project the image of the authors and designers. Even when the textbook deals with an apparently neutral or exact science, the author's perception is evident. And when this image contradicts that of the student, and by omission, maltreatment, or under-emphasis on culture or tradition makes the student feel unequal, a sense of inferiority develops. A chain reaction leading to mental slavery is now set in motion. Since most textbooks and teaching material are imported from the West, and the curriculum is modelled on western systems, the students' immediate environment is not acknowledged. Young biologists in the Muslim world dissect imported frogs even though rats can be found in abundance. In the fields of the humanities and social sciences, the fact that the history, culture and the world–view of the student may have contributed anything to the reservoir of global knowledge is not emphasized. It is an indictment of this education system that if you were to ask a university graduate anywhere in the Muslim world the simple question of whom he/she considered the greatest writer who had ever lived the immediate answer would be Shakespeare. Yet that student would have great difficulty in naming a literary representative of the local language.

The third element that subverts the emergence of relevant images is science and technology. The accepted characterization of science presents a picture of cooperative activity of independent producers of scientific information, offering their results freely to colleagues and members of the 'international scientific culture' renouncing the 'property' rights that an inventor protects in a patent and retaining only the prestige that accrues to a discovery.[13] Muslim countries have been duped totally by this image which ignores the fact that property relations can obstruct the free flow of scientific information as in the priority disputes, sharing of credit in team research, and rather feudal relationships between supervisors, assistants and research students. It is appreciated even less that the necessary modifications of the conventional image to fit present conditions involves multinational corporations which own scientific information along with patents, designs, copyrights, trade marks and physical assets. The corporately-owned scientific information is then deployed like any other sort of software, for the advantage of the company. In public establishments, and many commercial ones, it may eventually be released more or less freely for publication. But, in every case it is corporate property, rather than a free offering by a scientist.

The social importance of this new sector of science is now great and growing. The old-fashioned independent small-scale scientist does not usually make the discoveries that are directly translated into new processes and devices and he is never in a position to do the costly research and development work on his own. That requires large–scale resources, and a corporate decision in which scientists may share but will not dominate.

We see that the prevalent image in the Muslim countries of how science functions is a complete inversion of reality. Given this reality, those in the developing countries who wish to have access to some aspect of scientific information cannot simply go to the 'fountain of facts' and scoop up their requirements. Instead, they are likely to need access to the private property of some corporation. To obtain this may involve hard cash as well as sophisticated diplomacy. The gap between the idealized conventional image of freely available scientific information and the reality of close-fisted multinational corporations and secrecy-sensitive governments is a wide one.

The acceptance of the conventional image of science has two profound consequences for Muslim countries. As science is seen as a universally available free reservoir of knowledge, indigenous research and development is considered unnecessary, indeed a waste of resources. Moreover, while latest scientific results are freely and universally available, what need is there for preserving and indeed researching into centuries-old techniques and exploring traditional sources of knowledge?

Under such circumstances, technology transfer is promoted as the only viable alternative. The technological information that is needed by a Muslim country is usually protected by patents. The exporters set the price, what they will sell, when and where it will be delivered. The buyer therefore has no way of assessing the true financial, social or developmental costs of the purchased technology. Then there may be a number of strings and adverse conditions: compulsory purchase of other quite irrelevant products, restriction on exports of products that are manufactured by means of the purchased technology, restriction on the purchase of manufacturing components and competitive technologies; demands that custom duties and charges shall not be made, limitations on the development of local technical facilities; and compulsory sale of the manufactured product to the exporter at prices far below world market prices. With this framework, it is hardly surprising that technology transfer has led the Muslim countries further into dependency.

Even when there are a few tangible benefits to be derived from the transferred technology there are important factors which it does not deal with:

1. The collection of data on the availability of natural resources and the development of means to utilize these natural resources;
2. The particular conditions prevailing in Muslim countries, especially in agriculture and mineral production;
3. The development of processing methods suitable for the particular raw materials available locally;
4. The further development of modern technologies already installed in the country.[14]

What technology transfer does achieve is a transformation in the self-image of the local engineers. As Clement Henry Moore points out in his study of Egyptian engineers, *Image of Development*, imported technology carried an aura of prestige and glamour with it. Thus those engineers who were dealing with imported technology enjoyed a better image and higher status than those tackling local problems with local technology.

> As these technologies did not evolve from Egypt's previous efforts to industrialise, few Egyptians, however advanced their theoretical qualifications, enjoyed a working familiarity with them. Egypt lacked the intellectual as well as industrial infrastructure capable of integrating them into its economy. The showcase industries, such as iron and steel or automobile assembly, tended to be enclaves in a modern sector largely centered on the construction, textile, and food-processing industries. By importing the new technologies, the state enhanced the status of the engineers and gave some of them an opportunity to acquire new experience, but it perhaps also increased their dependence on the foreigners who had master-minded it. Apparently, the experiences with new technologies were not generating applied research, adapting and integrating them to local conditions; rather new forms of dependence on foreign experts were becoming self-perpetuating and were discouraging indigenous research.[15]

With indigenous research thwarted by promotion of images of glamour and sophistication, it is naturally not possible to develop the vast manpower of Muslim countries to its fullest advantage. If we presume that there is a similar proportionate distribution of the intellectual talent required for research work between all nations, long term moratoria on indigenous development of science and technology in the Muslim world means that its population is condemned to a level of intellectual activity well below their natural potential. The warning of Ivan Illich now takes on an ominous tone:

People who submit to the standards of others for the measure of their own personal growth soon apply the same ruler to themselves. They no longer have to be put in their place, but put themselves into their assigned slots, squeeze themselves into the niche which they have been taught to seek, and, in the very process, put their fellows into their places too, until everybody and everything fits.[16]

Political elites, the educational system and the conventional picture of science and technology play important parts in creating the image of dependency and helplessness in the Muslim countries. To a very large extent, introducing basic needs orientated development strategies in the Muslim world involves a conflict with the dominant images and enhancement of the traditional image that Muslim people have of themselves, their societies and civilization.

The role of information in promoting a strategy for development that aims at self-reliance and community participation, social justice and cultural authenticity centres on one hitherto unexplored activity: to preserve and convey traditions and traditional images in their original form. As Belkin and Robertson point out, to influence people's images without their consent and knowledge is unethical.[17] Considering that much of the information profession, wittingly or unwittingly, undermines the images of traditional societies, it is operating in an unethical capacity. It is the responsibility of the professional information scientist to ensure that information and knowledge on traditions, traditional cultures and traditional world-view filters down to the level of individual citizens. Moreover, modern knowledge and contemporary innovations have to be presented and conveyed to the citizens in a manner that does not weaken the existing cultural establishment. In a basic needs orientated strategy, information has to play a dual role. It has to preserve (not just in 'museum form' but in a dynamic, thriving, operationalized form) and upgrade folk cultures and their methods of knowing, doing and being. It has also to introduce innovations which enhance the notions of self-reliance and community participation, social justice and cultural authenticity in traditional societies in a way that does not undermine the customary images and subvert traditional culture. This means that those dealing with information have to equip themselves with the long lost notion of wisdom (*hikma*) — the goal at the other end of the information spectrum.

Notes

1. The reverse is also true. The industrialized countries have an image, propagated so well by Oxfam and Christian Aid posters, of the people of the

Third World. *Vide* Stig Findholm, *The Image of the Developing Countries*, Almquist and Wiksell, Stockholm, 1971.

2. Kenneth Boudling, The Image, University of Michigan Press, Ann Arbor, 1961.

3. Edward Said, *Orientalism*, Routledge and Kegan Paul, London, 1978. See also his essay 'Orientalism Reconsidered' in *Arab Society*, Samih K. Farsoun (ed.), Croom Helm, London, 1985; and A.L. Tibawi, *English Speaking Orientalists*, Islamic Culture Centre, London, 1965.

4. Parvez Manzoor, 'Eunuchs in the Harem of History', *Inquiry*, **2** (1) 39–46 (1985).

5. Leon Uris, *Haj*, Corgi, 1985.

6. Phillip Caputo, *Horn of Africa*, Futura, London, 1982; see also the brilliant review by Khurram Murad, 'We the Civilized, *They* the Barbarians', *Muslim World Book Review*, **6** (3) 3–14 (1986).

7. Daniel Pipes, *In the Path of God*, Basic Books, New York, 1984; see also Parvez Manzoor's review which thoroughly demolishes Pipes in *Muslim World Book Review*, **6** (4) 17–19 (1986).

8. John Laffin, *The Dagger of Islam*, Sphere Books, London, 1979.

9. Ronald C. Benge, *Cultural Crisis and Libraries in the Third World*, Clive Bingley, London, 1979, p. 53.

10. *ibid.*, p. 54.

11. *ibid.*, p. 57.

12. Hasan Fathy makes this point forcefully in his classic study, *Architecture for the Poor*, University of Chicago Press, 1973.

13. For a detailed discussion of this point see J.R. Ravetz, *Scientific Knowledge and its Social Problems*, Oxford University Press, 1972; Paul Feyerabend, *Science in a Free Society*, Verso, London, 1978; and W.H. Newton-Smith, *The Rationality of Science*, Routledge and Kegan Paul, London, 1981.

14. For further discussion and an analysis of the adverse effect of transfer of technology see M.Taghi Farver and John P. Milton, *The Careless Technology*, Natural History Press, New York, 1972; and Ziauddin Sardar, *Science, Technology and Development in the Muslim World*, Croom Helm, London, 1979.

15. Clement Henry Moore, *Images of Development*, MIT Press, Cambridge, Massachusetts, 1980, p. 97-8.

16. Ivan Illich, *Deschooling Society*, Boyars, London, 1973, p. 45.

17. N.J. Belkin and S.E. Robertson, 'Some Ethical and Political Implications of Theoretical Research in Information Science', paper presented at ASIS Annual Meeting, 1976; quoted by B.J. Kostrewski and Charles Oppenheim, 'Ethics in Information Science', *Journal of Information Science*, **1**(5) 277-83 (1980).

6

Citizens and Peasants

Information and the Quality of Life

The domination of certain images in Muslim countries has meant that the information needs of some sectors of society have been completely ignored. Indeed, it was assumed until quite recently that it was only scientists, technologists and decision-makers who need information; ordinary citizens, rural areas and inner-city poor had no need of information. But information is something that is required by all segments of society: citizens and peasants, professionals and decision-makers, scientists and technologists, scholars and intellectuals. Moreover, all these constituent elements of society require different kinds of information in different forms. It is therefore necessary both to assess what kind of information each part of society needs and develop appropriate means of delivery for it.

The Prophet of Islam has been reported to have said that the believers are like a body, if one part of the body catches an infection, the whole body suffers. If we take the Muslim world to be a body, a holistic system, then we know that every activity of this body must be coordinated. We also know that each activity requires an internal flow of information between the parts. We have brains primarily so that we can coordinate our bodily activities with our left hand acting in conjunction with our right hand. Coordination and integration have long been recognized in physiology as the highest function of the brain. However, systems of other types, not least holistic systems, also need coordination which leads to integration, makes optimum use of scarce resources and lays the foundation for self-development. Big cities, for example, need schematized traffic laws; the prevention of pollution requires that many preventive and remedial actions operate in conjunction; and in social problems too the activities of welfare agencies need to be harmonized.

Coordination is basically an holistic phenomenon, discernible only in the whole. Let us illustrate this by giving the example of the classic type of coordination shown by the tight-rope walker. His four limbs must always be in a position to maintain his centre of gravity over the wire. The unskilled person may well be able to move his limbs as well as the experienced tight-rope walker, but the unskilled person will use a combination of positions, all four limbs to the left say, that the experienced walker would avoid. Thus the contrast between the unskilled and the skilled may be shown by the fact that the skilled confines his actions to a particular subset of those automatically possible. What is the relevance of the tight-rope walker to the Muslim world? The present relationship between developed and developing countries has placed the Muslim world on a delicately balanced tight-rope. Whether we manage to walk to the safety of self-reliance and self-development of Islam will depend on our skill as well as the coordination of our activities. When the tight-rope walker takes a false step he immediately re-adjusts his centre of gravity using a feedback of information. Within the Muslim world, there is an acute need for such self-correcting mechanisms.

The free transmission of information is essential in the development of such self-corrective, holistic systems. If 'the believers are like a body', then the free flow of information is essential for the survival of this body. In other words, the notion of the *ummah* does not really make sense unless there is unrestrained intercommunication, as a consequence of which it behaves as a coordinated body. The free flow of information is also essential for the growth of a decision structure and the maintenance of order and organization in a society. With unchecked internal movement of information, interactive holistic systems thrive. No part of the system then has unilateral control over the remainder or any other part. The characteristics of the system are inherent in the ensemble as a whole. Thus the survival and the stability of the Muslim world depends on the relationship between various Muslim countries — the subsystems — and the level of cooperation and coordination that they can develop; and for individual Muslim countries, appropriate emphasis on rural and urban areas is an important factor for achieving an autonomous and independent status. The Islamic consciousness of the Muslim world comprehends it as a whole. When we view the Muslim world as an interactive, holistic system we see that there is no place in it for paternalism, let alone domination by one country over another, or one segment of the community over another. The system demands sharing of experience and information, cooperation between scientific, technical and commercial fields, and coordination of activities on a national and international level — in fact, the system needs the operational form of the concept of *Shura* (cooperation for the good). Without free movement of information within the Muslim world, and within individual nations, there cannot be a common perception, or a common vision, or even coordination or integration; and the notion of *ijma*, the Islamic recommendation of developing a consensus within the community, makes little sense. And without a spirit of cooperation and coordination and a common vision it is not easy to walk on a tight-rope. Unlike the tightrope walker, Muslim countries do not have a safety net.

It is a truism to state that information is power. The truism takes on more force in its opposite form. Without information — without opportunity to select, distribute and discuss information — one has no power. Those who lack information are often the most conscious of this relationship. When information is allowed to flow freely within a society, it provides an access to power for the 'have-nots' and checks the concentration of power in fewer and fewer hands. It thus serves *istislah* (public interest) and promotes *adl*, (justice). When the free flow of information is checked, it is used for paternalism and domination, *zulm* (tyranny) and not *adl* is thus promoted. Information thus plays a vital role in a society and can be used to enhance the quality of life in a community or by withholding and controlling it, it can become a tool of despotism and social injustice.

Our information on contemporary rural and urban environment is highly incomplete. Not only are we unable to evaluate the alternatives that we face, but we are not even aware of a high percentage of them. The speed of the transmission of stimuli and the volume of new information has increased, but the limitations of individuals to receive that information has become more marked relative to society as a whole. *Per se* there is no indication that individual genius or perception have changed in any important manner, for better or worse, in the last few centuries. However, the output of information, the rate of change, and the complexity of society have increased by many orders of magnitude. In such circumstances maintaining and improving the quality of life becomes a permanent issue. Information plays an important part in unveiling the complexities of modern life as well as in the dissemination and building up of individual and social *hikma*.

If information can be used to promote such basic concepts of the

world-view of Islam as *tawheed, adl, shura, ijma, istislah,* and *hikma,*
what would be the more specific aims of an information policy based on
these values? Information policies geared to improving the quality of life
should aim at providing:

1. Services by which citizens can develop their ability to participate in
   national decision-making processes.
2. Mechanisms by which individuals and communities should be able
   to consult and cooperate on matters of common concern.
3. Services that provide free and easy access to information for citizens
   on matters that affect them such as legal rights, environmental issues,
   national and public policy concerns and on matters which would help
   communities face everyday problems.

The provision of these services and mechanisms are essential for
making any improvements in the quality of life in Muslim societies.
Such services would raise the literacy and educational levels and would
foster the emergence of a communal, national and civilizational image in
the Muslim world. To a large extent, developing the ability of citizens to
participate in national decision-making processes means fighting illiteracy. In most parts of the Muslim world the illiteracy rate is well over
80 per cent, and in some countries, for example, Afghanistan and Mali,
it is over 90 per cent. On this scale, it is a deep narcotic in the consciousness of the *ummah*. For each illiterate individual it is a token of
subservience, non-participation and separation from creative effort and
the realization of *shura, ijma* and *hikma*. Illiteracy is a great curtain
preventing millions of people from entering the creative life of the
modern world of which the printed word is a chart. The curtain is, as it
were, a thick glass through which the illiterate can peer darkly. They can
see the national activities in progress but cannot share in them. They can
see the impressive equipment of modern life but cannot reach out to use
them, much less to control them. But once awareness comes of the
power of the things beyond the curtain, a deep frustration sets in; a
frustration that can lead to lethargy and impotence.

Those who are exposed to the mass media, driven by advertising, the
sole purpose of which is to break through our protection against the
crushing overload of urban sensation, may be tempted to envy the
illiterate in his more organic world. Whereas we have become slaves to
time, machine and organization, the illiterate is a slave to his incapacity,
his societal impotence, his suffocation. For him, the world is a hostile
environment, terrifying in its dependence upon words.

For a Muslim country, a large illiterate population means the loss of its major resource, human potential. Moreover, illiteracy also enforces oligarchic, tyrannical and imperial power and can be one of the chief means by which such power is maintained. Experience teaches us that programmes of functional literacy succeed only when they are coupled to library and information policies as well as social and economic planning programmes. Indeed, as the title of Edward Carter's essay suggests, *Literacy, Libraries and Liberty*, these elements are closely interrelated. Literacy has no operative dimension unless there are things to read, and one has freedom to read everything from books to newspapers, magazines to posters:

> From our literate citadel we are justified in thinking that a country's reading provides an accurate reflection of its social and cultural state, and so it does with two big qualifications. In a partially literate country the reflection can be only partial, and in any country which has failed to develop its own indigenous authorship and a publishing industry to serve it, the reflection will be distorted by the power of countries with active book export programmes to impose their alien cultures. Perhaps my metaphor is wrong. The influence of aggressive alien book import programmes is not just to distort the reflection but to distort the character and form of the people themselves.[1]

Public Libraries and Public Service

Libraries designed to meet the needs of rural and urban poor, ethnic minorities and specific cultural groups are one of the most potent weapons for fighting illiteracy and improving the educational standards of a population. In Muslim countries, the library is one of the most neglected national institutions; only Egypt, Turkey, Pakistan, Iraq, Saudi Arabia, Iran and Malaysia have public libraries. Moreover, the few libraries that do exist tend to be rather passive institutions. They neither take an active part in illiteracy campaigns nor act to create group consciousness. The existing libraries in Muslim countries are largely a colonial legacy and operate much as libraries operated in nineteenth-century Britain; being based on the assumption of universal literacy in the English language, as well as minimum income level, common culture and class interests. It was only natural that colonial regimes evolved the same structure when setting up libraries in pre-independent Muslim states where they were meant to cater only for the needs of government bureaucracy and expatriate settlers. After independence, these libraries were capable of meeting the needs of only the ruling elites.

Libraries in Muslim societies have consciously to break this colonial link. Moreover, they cannot continue to be passive institutions expecting the user to come to them. If they are to serve any relevant function in development, public libraries in Muslim societies must become dynamic social institutions, an integral part of the physical equipment of Islamic culture. And the librarian should not simply serve as a mediator between the community and the stock of information the library possesses but become an active agent in fighting illiteracy, social oppression and developing self-reliance and self-sufficiency in communities. The librarian's job is not limited to being confined by the physical space of his/her institution but requires going out into the community and being involved with the forces of change and community development. This requires a drastic change in the self-image of librarians. In Muslim societies, there is a strange social stigma attached to service and service professions. The concept of service connotes menial work and is not considered to be the province of an educated person such as the librarian. This absurd notion must be rejected; and librarians should see community service and involvement as an integral part of their profession.

In addition to public libraries, Muslim societies need two other kinds of information agencies. There is a need for agencies relating specifically to consumer information; and there is also the need for a more specialized information agency which can provide access to more general information which can help members of a community face daily, though often complex, problems. These may range from a simple need to get medical advice and help to a more sophisticated desire for a deeper insight into local political issues.

Appropriate consumer information is essential if the hold of the superior image of imported goods is to be tackled. Consumers in Muslim societies prefer to buy inferior, often harmful, imported products at inflated prices than purchase better, cheaper and more appropriate, locally produced alternatives. Some local alternatives would be available almost free; but the image of inferiority associated with them means that they are ignored, which in turn, leads to the collapse of local industry and dependence on imported goods. The malpractices of multinational companies in the Muslim countries are well documented; their products may come with slick images, but often lead to long-term harmful effects for the consumer. The controversy surrounding powdered milk versus breast milk illustrates the point well. The Consumer Association of Penang (CAP), Malaysia, which has pioneered the dissemination of consumer information to citizens, argues that competition amongst importers and suppliers is so intense that it often leads to fraudulent malpractices which are used unscrupulously in an attempt to secure a larger share of the market. 'Misleading advertisements, aggressive sales techniques aimed at emotively appealing to the consumer, false labelling, unfair pricing are examples of some common malpractices.' In addition, the multinational habit of dumping dangerous goods which have been banned in Europe and America, means that consumers have found themselves eating food with harmful additives, colouring matter and preservatives, using dangerous chemicals or have been persuaded to buy products that perform no useful function. CAP argues along the following lines:

> It is therefore imperative that consumers, especially those in the lower-income categories be made more aware of how *vulnerable* they are. The vast majority of our population constitutes households who cannot afford any wasteful or misdirected consumption . . . Consumers must therefore become more aware of their basic rights — namely the right to be adequately informed, the right to products which will not endanger their safety and good health and the right to be heard and redressed . . . Awareness of rights alone is not enough. Consumers must develop a critical capacity for evaluation and decision. They must know where and how to seek accurate information.[2]

CAP's chosen method of informing Malaysian citizens is the production of consumer orientated newspapers which are published in local languages (and sell in hundreds of thousands) and frequent seminars which the Association organizes throughout the country. There are, however, other methods that can be used for communicating consumer information. Radio and television are used largely for entertainment in the Muslim world; their vast potential for communicating consumer and other information has not been explored. Moreover, video films are in extensive use — even the most remote village tends to have a video machine or two which are used to provide entertainment for the entire village. In cities, certain cafes and restaurants have videos which are used to entertain and attract customers. These outlets could be used to inform these captive audiences with specially and cheaply prepared videos of consumer information. Consumer information services, on the lines of CAP, are essential in Muslim countries, both to provide self-confidence in locally produced goods and safeguard the interests of consumers from the exploitative practices of foreign companies.

For providing a more general service designed to help members of a community face their complex everyday problems, community information and referral services (CIRs) are needed. In most Muslim countries, when community members face a problem, they often do not know where to turn for help. Often, after knocking on one bureaucratic door after another, they end up frustrated and in despair. CIRs would cater for people in this position. They could play important roles not just in guiding local communities towards proper channels of information but also in helping communities develop their understanding of how local and central government agencies and organizations function and therefore in gaining a fuller understanding of their services. They would help in the acquisition of information, facts and statistics to argue against, and if necessary, to combat the bureaucratic machinery; and they would foster a sense of involvement in community life.

CIRs can be located in public libraries. Since these are often nonexistent, it may be necessary to find alternative avenues for the establishment of these much needed services. CIRs need not be big institutions: a small collection of specialized literature, with, where possible and desirable, a microcomputer with appropriate data base, and well-trained staff is all that is needed. The setting up of CIRs in every community district should be the goal in any serious proposals about providing access to relevant information in urban and rural areas. The small cost of setting up these institutions does not compare with the overall gains that can be derived in improving citizen participation and awareness in a country.

Moreover, CIRs can also bring dividends for governments and local authorities themselves. They can be used for collecting data about the patterns of problems in a community.and how these change. They can serve as sensitive barometers of the quality of life of a community. The technique by which CIRs involve themselves in community life to reflect accurately their needs, and by which they collect and record reliable data, organize and analyse it — all these methods can be used to provide policy-makers with background information for developing their policies. Once the policy is formulated, the same techniques can be used to assess the extent to which the policy actually works, and the extent to which it is effecting the desired changes in the community. The simplest technique is to monitor continuously indicators of the quality of life such as improvements in literacy, awareness of legal rights, participation in national issues and communal cohesion. On a more sophisticated level, CIRs can try to detect unusual patterns in community development likely to reveal changes in the quality of life.

There is one other form of information service which has a direct bearing, although not widely recognized, on the life-style of a country — the indigenous publishing industry. Wide availability of books and quality magazines are essential for the free flow of information. Unfortunately, the publication industry is almost non-existent in most Muslim countries; and what does exist tends to cater for the lowest common denominator rather than working to improve the quality of national literature and thought. Decision-makers, scholars and intellectuals, as well as professional librarians and information scientists have to work together to develop a solid indigenous publication industry in every Muslim country. Both the lack of quality reading material, as well as the import of books from the industrialized countries, is culturally and intellectually subversive. Moreover, the lack of an indigenous publication industry thwarts the development of local intellectual and literary talent and eventually ends up eradicating the national talent pool.

The absence of a local publication industry is one reason why there are so few libraries in the Muslim world. If an overwhelming proportion of the library stock has to be imported, with hard cash, then libraries become an expensive enterprise. The lack of libraries and unavailability of literature mean that the average citizen in Muslim countries does not develop a habit of reading and, as such, never develops an open mind and attitudes that can appreciate and understand differences of opinions and views. Self-expression is suppressed not just because there are no channels of outlet but also because many citizens are not aware that they have anything to express!

One advantage of the new information technologies is that they make the production of books and magazines easier and cheaper. It is now possible for an average entrepreneur to become a one-man publishing enterprise. Within the next decade, developments in microcomputer typesetting and printing technology will become even more accessible. The positive features of this technology should be exploited to establish thriving, local publication industries in Muslim countries.

Delivering Information to Rural Areas

The bulk of the population of the Muslim world lives in the rural areas and it is their needs relating to agriculture and basic survival which are most conspicuously overlooked by the existing information systems. A major problem in disseminating information to rural areas is illiteracy; as most villagers cannot read, the printed word is of limited use. The use of audiovisual material therefore takes on more significance.

Rural populations tend to have strong oral traditions. No attempt is made even by national or public libraries to collect and document the highly relevant and useful information that exists in the collective memory of village dwellers, this having been tested for particular local conditions by generation after generation and having passed into oral folklore after proving its worth. It is essential that such information is documented and that the oral medium is used effectively both to communicate and disseminate information. While it may not be possible to establish a library in every village, it is possible to supply a tape recorder to most villages to record their stock of information and use it to communicate information on pre-recorded audio-tapes.

The use of radio for communicating information to rural areas is surprisingly ignored in most Muslim countries. The radio is used largely to provide entertainment and news for the urban elite and most of the broadcasts are in the national language. But rural communities are often monoglot in local languages. In Pakistan, for example, rural communities speak different languages, none of which bears even a passing resemblance to the national language, Urdu. Broadcasts in Urdu are, not surprisingly, ignored by most rural populations. Shiraz Durrani's comment on the use of radio in Kenya, applies equally well to most Muslim countries:

> Even if the language barriers were to be overcome, the content of most radio-broadcasts leaves much to be desired. The emphasis is once again on entertainment for the educated elite in the towns. A certain number of hours are devoted to educational broadcasts for adults and schools, but the content of these is also far removed from the struggles of the peasants. *The* only broadcasts that cater for farmers are those prepared by the Agriculture Information Centre. These, however, are not sufficiently frequent to have any real impact. Again they do not allow for regional variations, as they are broadcast nationally to areas with totally different climates, land use and agricultural practices. In addition, there is a tendency for such broadcasts to encourage the use of the so-called 'modern' technologies without considering their appropriateness in the local situation. Peasants have rejected many of these methods as being unsuitable for them, having suffered large losses in the past. In order to win back the confidence of the peasants, such broadcasts will have to promote only those technologies which have been proved useful for the peasants in their *shambas*, not in the Ministry's classroom and laboratories'[3]

Imposing information from the top onto rural communities is not only unjust, but counter-productive. Moreover, agriculture is intrinsically linked to life-style: asking peasants to change their farming practices amounts to asking them to change their way of living. If one considers the spectacular failure of high- technology agriculture in the Third World, and the misery, drop in productivity and the resultant underdevelopment that technological wonders such as the Green Revolution have caused, the wisdom of traditional agriculture and the life-style associated with it, cannot be denied.[4] It is now widely accepted that agricultural productivity in Muslim societies, and in the Third World in general, can be increased only by upgrading the traditional systems thereby making them more efficient. Since there is virtually no information on traditional methods of agriculture and irrigation, the first task before planners in Muslim societies is to learn from the peasants themselves. This means that rural and agricultural information systems must have strong inputs from the rural populations.

In a study of the provision of agricultural information in Nigeria, Lenrie Aina points out that 95 per cent of rural farmers in Nigeria obtain their information through personal contacts.[5] What is true of Nigeria is largely true of all Muslim countries. To facilitate adequate communication and appropriate two-way transfer of information between rural populations and agricultural planners and researchers, there is a need to establish a permanent link: each rural locality needs to have a full-time agricultural information and extension officer who both gathers information from the farmers as well as supplies them with adequate and relevant information. Without this permanent personal channel of communication, researchers can neither learn from the peasants nor pass on adequate information to them at appropriate times.

To fulfil other information needs of rural communities, rural libraries have to be established. Up to now no attention has been paid to establishing village libraries in Muslim countries. However, it is not necessary that every village should have a library; what is essential is that it has access to one. The first step in this regard is setting up district libraries with facilities to reach the rural areas. Indeed, village libraries cannot be established *en masse* in an entire country without central libraries in major districts. These district libraries can be used to service a network of mobile libraries which visit remote areas on a regular basis. Well-stocked district libraries can administer and efficiently service as well as replenish the bookstocks of mobile libraries. Mobile libraries in conjunction with static village and district libraries can reach a vast number of scattered populations. Moreover, they can also be of service to rural schools most of which do not have library facilities. That such libraries ought to emphasize audio-visual material, including the recording of books on tapes, need not be repeated.

Without adequately fulfilling the information needs of rural areas, a basic needs orientated strategy for development cannot be implemented. It is the rural areas that provide most of the basic foodstuffs of Muslim countries, and it is in the rural areas that most of their manpower lives. If the basic needs of the rural areas remain unfulfilled, genuine development cannot take place; under such circumstances any talk of self-reliance and self-sufficiency is clearly absurd.

However, the total quality of life in Muslim societies can improve only if both the information needs of the rural areas as well as of the inner city poor are understood and appropriately met. The evolution of a network of village and mobile libraries in Muslim countries must go hand-in-hand with the setting up of dynamic public libraries, consumer information systems, community information and referral services and the emergence of a broad based, thriving indigenous publication industry. To a large extent, all these institutions are dependent on each other and complement each other's services. The flowering of these institutions in Muslim societies will not only enable us to express practically the basic values of the world-view of Islam, improve coordination and cooperation between urban and rural areas, promote creativity and intellectual development, but will also lay the foundation for the re-emergence of a dynamic and thriving Muslim civilization of the future.

Notes

1. Edward Carter, *Literacy, Libraries and Liberty*, Library Association, London, 1969, p. 13.
2. Consumer Association of Penang, *Consumer Education*, Penang, 1977, p. 3.
3. Shiraz Durrani, 'Rural Information in Kenya', *Information Development*, **1** (3) 149–157 (1985).
4. See Claude Alvares, 'The Green Revolution: An Obituary', *Inquiry*, **3** (3) 44–9 (1986).
5. Lenrie O. Aina, 'Agricultural Information Provision in Nigeria', *Information Development*, **2** (4) 242–4 (1986).

7

Scientists and Scholars

Transfer of Information or Communication of Knowledge?

The re-emergence of a dynamic, thriving Muslim civilization of the future is a direct function of the creativity and intellectual development of Muslim scientists, scholars and intellectuals. The responsibility for solving the complex and inter-related array of contemporary problems that face Muslim societies rests largely on their shoulders. Moreover, without their sustained efforts a basic needs orientated strategy for development cannot be translated into a practical reality. To a very large extent, this means that they have to introduce components of self-reliance and community participation into their work and make social justice and cultural authenticity a cornerstone of their thought.

At present, neither Muslim scientists nor scholars are in a position to carry out their responsibilities and become the leading architects for reconstructing the Muslim civilization of our time. Both science and scholarship in the Muslim world are at a nadir. But while there are indications that Muslim scholarship is regaining some of its originality and dynamism, science and technology in the Muslim world continues to lack self-expression and originality. It is sporadic, isolated, largely unconnected with local needs and quite incapable of self-sustenance. Lack of ideas, imagination and self-expression is one reason for the present state of science in the Muslim world; I have described this condition in detail elsewhere.[1] But there is another, equally important reason, for this present lamentable state: the acute lack of adequate and appropriate information structures to serve scientists and technologists and the poor communication of science within the Muslim world. Behind both these reasons there is a single cause: the way science and scientific and technological information is perceived in Muslim countries.

Muslim intellectuals, social scientists, natural scientists, architects, planners and decision-makers believe that if they had access to information sources in the industrialized countries, they would become more professional and more productive. The transfer of information to the Muslim world is perceived on a similar basis as the transfer of technology: Muslim countries, for the last three decades, have been buying ready-made, off-the-shelf technology from the industrialized North, and they realize that they can buy information on the same basis. The image at work here is that all science is good and relevant, and all scientific and technological information reduces uncertainty and leads to productivity of scientific and technologial enterprise. Much of the energy of information scientists, librarians and their organizations and institutions is spent in promoting this image and setting up systems which enable the transfer of information to take place.

When trying to acquire information from the industrialized countries Muslim information scientists face a daunting task. Much of the difficulty arises from the fact that both science itself and scientific information systems are facing a crisis. The steady exponential growth of occidental science has produced quantitative problems for the communication as well as the transfer of scientific information. There are over 90,000 journals in the scientific and technical category, and twice this number with some relevant information. Specialization of journals by content, even if not always by title, is severe. The old ambition of being generally aware of developments in all scientific areas can no longer be realized. Even to keep fully abreast of what is happening in one field, as defined in nineteenth-century terms, is becoming an impossibility. University departments which may be labelled in broad terms tend to split into sets of micro-specialist sub-divisions. The task of training students to be competent for research even in a sub-discipline is all too daunting and even narrower specialization ensues.

The cumulative effects of these developments can be serious. Today's leading scientists are aware of the fragmentation of science, because they were taught by men who had memories of an age when broad views and synthesis were possible and encouraged. Tomorrow's students are in danger of losing a personal link with the period when research in natural science aspired to be a learned enquiry, rather than a technique. Despite all the brave words of the philosophers of science, there is no guarantee that science will continue to be a creative and humane venture. It would be all too easy for scientists to respond to the apparent overload of information by cultivating and then believing in a narrow puzzle-solving approach to research. Should that occur, the contribution of scientific research to civilization will inevitably diminish. It would also be more difficult to educate scientists and citizens so that they become competent to manage the new problems posed by science and technology in a finite world.

Western scientists are now faced with the possibility that the exceedingly rapid growth, apparently regulated only by occidental, external constraints, has been taking science to the limits of a viable size as a communication system. Organisms deprived of their natural growth regulators can grow beyond a size that their structure and metabolism can maintain. There is no apparent reason why intellectual systems should be immune from such a condition.

The conventional solutions for the problem of information explosion are all envisaged as an improved shuttle of information between producers and consumers, with better mechanisms for signalling and transfer. The problem of information — discord and the fragmentation of scientific knowledge — are not seen as anything outside the capabilities of a computer and on-line data bases. However, this over-emphasis on information technologies leads to neglect of other important parts of the problem. For example, there are large areas of scientific research where the principle that science is public property with open access to research, does not apply, and where information shuttles are of no help to those who need the information. In these areas of science the genuine problem of information — discord between the producer and the consumer — is aggravated by information-blockage. As many of the social and environmental problems of science relate to research which is the 'private property' of multi-national corporations and governments, neglect of information-blockage here impedes any recognition and solution of these urgent problems of the communication of scientific data.[2]

When Muslim librarians and information scientists manage to overcome the problems of information transfer, they discover that much of the information acquired from the industrialized countries — in the form of scientific papers, technical reports, social surveys, urban masterplans, educational advice, models of social and institutional management, and so on — turns out to be irrelevant. Muslim scientists, technologists, social activists, urban planners and policy makers find that these bits of information, data and advice are far removed from their reality. In other words, when this information is integrated with the value system and cultural concerns of Muslim societies, it fails to meet the criteria of useful, appropriate knowledge. It fails to solve the many, acute and pressing problems of Muslim societies. It leads not to the reduction of uncertainty and increase in ability to solve problems, but an increase in uncertainty and a consequent decrease in the ability to solve problems. Indeed, most often this information aggravates these problems and generates a host of new ones thus leading to the erosion of cherished values and the confidence that Muslims have in their own culture and tradition.

However, all this is not surprising. The generation of the increasing spiral of information and new technologies is concentrated in a handful of rich, industrial countries. In approximate terms, the United States is responsible for about one-third of world-wide expenditure on research and development. Western Europe and Japan account for another third. And the Soviet Union and Eastern Europe spend just under one-third of the total. This means that the developing countries of Asia, Africa and Latin America account for only a miniscule fraction of the world's research and development activities: less than 3 per cent. Thus 97 per cent of the world's research and development information output generated by all this activity is geared, naturally, to the needs and requirements of the producer societies. It does not reflect the priorities of Muslim societies.[3]

It has been shown that the priorities of developed nations are almost diametrically opposed to the problems faced by developing countries. Colin Norman, for example, points out that almost a quarter of the global research on development expenditure goes on military goals. He writes:

> Military R and D alone accounts for more financial and intellectual resources than are devoted to R and D on health, food production, energy, and environmental protection combined. Moreover, as the global distribution of R and D capacity implies, the world's research and development enterprise is overwhelmingly geared to meeting the political and economic goals of the industrial nations. These priorities, which differ from country to country, are the result of a constellation of forces. The global research and development budget is the product of vested interests, whether they be corporations seeking higher profits, governments seeking greater military and political strength, or university scientists seeking larger research budgets.[4]

Moreover, even research in areas such as health brings no real benefits to Muslim societies. For example, the US priorities in health are cancer, heart disease, obesity, new strains of sexual diseases such as herpes and AIDS, and heart, lung and liver transplants. In Bangladesh, however, the major killers are diarrhoea, malnutrition, TB and a new strain of cholera; other major diseases include filaria, leprosy, enteric fever and gastro-enteritis. Other Muslim countries have equally different priorities: Egypt faces an epidemic of bilharzia, in Sudan bilharzia and river blindness have reached unprecedented levels, and so on. When it comes to normative disciplines such as architecture and town planning the relevance of research carried out and information generated in industrialized countries fades into complete insignificance.

Moreover, it is not easy for Muslim countries to have access to that information which is relevant to their needs. Almost always Muslim countries find that the information which they perceive to be relevant is protected in one way or another. It is not surprising that in societies where information is the dominant economic activity, it is jealously guarded by those who possess it. The declaration of UNISIST II that 'scientific and technological information, together with economic, social and cultural information, constitutes a common asset of humanity' is only a pious hope.[5] In reality, it is a cruel hoax for information now plays the same role, and is protected with the same enthusiasm, as energy and capital. It is the key commodity and variable of modern society. In particular, scientific information is a major source of power.

Thus, the transfer of information from industrialized countries to Muslim countries not only introduces a great deal of irrelevant information, it also generates a dynamic of dependency. Consider a data system like MEDLAR which contains information on countless pharmaceutical drugs produced by multinational corporations. Extensive use of such systems induces reliance on foreign patented drugs which are not only expensive but in most cases quite useless and dangerous. When Bangladesh followed a basic needs orientated medical policy, it discovered that out of more than 5,000 patented drugs which were being sold in the country, only 200 could be described as essential. Moreover, many of the essential drugs could be produced locally or could be acquired cheaply in non-trade name formulations. But major information systems were geared to providing information on patented drugs with established trade names and information on the others was hard to come by. The consequences of this are obvious: diseases like TB, filaria and cholera remained uncontrolled but pharmaceutical activity in Bangladesh continued to increase. The principle reason for this horrendous state of affairs is the conversion of health into a major new frontier for the expansion of capital. Medical information systems are a key tool in the expansion of capital and strengthening the control of pharmaceutical multinationals on the Third World.[6]

The over-enthusiasm in Muslim countries for plugging into the research and development and information systems of industrialized countries has a number of dire consequences for science and technology in the Muslim world:

1. Science and technology acquires wrong priorities: for example, more emphasis is given to theoretical physics than food sciences. Essential fundamental research such as in agriculture, is sacrificed at the altar of more exotic and fashionable areas such as cancer research. The emphasis on transfer of technology reduces the importance of indigenous research on industrial issues.

2. Because the international system of science insists on perpetuating the myth that science and technology are 'neutral', Muslim scientists plugged into this system do not appreciate the philosophical, cultural and subjective dimension of the information they acquire from industrialized countries, or generate themselves within the framework of this system.

3. Because of its irrelevance, both indigenous research on western priorities and imported information do not serve the needs of Muslim societies. This generates distrust and tension between scientists and the society they are supposed to serve.

4. Even where emphasis is given to local needs and requirements, Muslim scientists seek justification for their work in the international system of research and development. Because this system either rejects this research as irrelevant or gives very, very low priority to research needs of Muslim countries, Muslim scientists have an extremely difficult time in getting published or earning recognition for their work. This generates an inferiority complex and sense of impotence amongst them.

5. Because of heavy reliance on the international system of science, Muslim scientists are caught in a vicious circle of information overload and poverty of information. On the one hand, they are awe struck at the amount of work done in the industrialized countries and the research output coming their way. On the other, the specific information that they need for their work is extremely hard to find. The too much and too little syndrome generates a sense of confusion.

6. Because they are always struggling to find information for their specific needs, and are cut off from other scientists working in their own area, Muslim scientists suffer from isolation and loneliness which stifles original thought and creativity.

These factors combine to produce the sorry state of science we find in the Muslim world. The undue reliance on the international channels of communication for science means that Muslim scientists and technologists and information scientists supporting them pay very little attention to promoting communication, contact and exchange of information within their national boundaries. Scientists within a Muslim country literally do not know what work is being done in the university or research centre a few miles away from their laboratory. Internal scientific communication is the life-blood of any indigenous scientific community. To be efficient and productive a scientist must be in contact with at least three other scientists at the same level and within the same discipline. This is the 'critical mass'; without this minimum contact there can be no exchange of results and ideas. When Muslim scientists are deprived of this contact, it is not surprising that suffocation, and the mediocrity that suffocation generates, is produced.

The over-emphasis on transfer of information from the industrialized countries also has serious consequences for the information resources in the Muslim world. Scarce manpower and financial resources are misdirected, producing a lack of coherence and coordination amongst information services. Salem identifies a number of shortcomings of information systems in the Arab world:

1. Lack of surveys of the information resources in Arab countries, coordination between them and provision of national plans.
2. Lack of coordination of information in Arab countries. Many organizations and institutions provide the same information service without regard to others, creating waste of time, manpower and money.
3. Lack of objective plans for information services to form a coordinated network.
4. Different use of library and information science terminology and different methods of applying cataloguing and classification rules.
5. Lack of communication with international information services provided by the United Nations agencies and international unions and societies.
6. Many of the Arab countries have not joined international standard systems such as the International Standard Book and Serial Numbers and copyright agreements.
7. Lack of appreciation of the importance of a national information infrastructure.
8. Shortage of professional manpower, training and education in information science and librarianship.[7]

What can be done to overcome these shortcomings? Moreover, what can be done to break out of the present impasse of science in the Muslim world? There is a single solution to both problems. Once we realize that, with the exception of certain basic sciences, the information generated in the industrialized countries is irrelevant in the strict sense of the word, the solution to the crisis of science in the Muslim world becomes obvious. The main issue for Muslim countries is not the transfer of information from the industrialized world but the generation of appropriate information in the Muslim world itself. And that means that *Muslim countries substantially must increase their expenditure for research and development.* Most Muslim countries spend even less than the mandatory one per cent of the GNP recommended by a number of international organizations. Indigenous research capability is not a question of luxury, or the pursuit of knowledge for the sake of knowledge, it is essential for solving the needs of the Muslim community, shaking off dependency and surviving in the contemporary world.

In addition to indigenous generation of information, Muslim countries have to develop their own network for the communication of science and intellectual endeavours. As I have argued, it is not just that Muslim scientists and intellectuals are completely marginalized from the international communication of science and thought, but this system is not geared to solving the needs and requirements of Muslim scientists and intellectuals. The need is for a communication system that pitches the work of Muslim scientists, scholars and thinkers at the international level of the *ummah*, increases contacts between like-minded thinkers and scientists working in the same area and provides them with a sense of confidence and achievement; a communication system that promotes the notions of *shura* and fosters *ijma* in the professional and intellectual Muslim community.

Information and Communication

At this point we must differentiate between the mere transfer of information and the actual process of communication. It is a common mistake to equate the transfer of information with communication. The two, of course, are quite different things.

Information transfer involves the shuttle of information from one place, the source of the originator, to another, the user. In this flow of information inevitably there is a loss, and sometimes even distortion of information. As Jason Farradane pointed out over two decades ago:

If information is transmitted in a shortened form, even in a carefully prepared report, there will be loss. In the form of an abstract, or, far worse, merely a title or a journal reference, the loss is large. The various forms of indexes used in information retrieval systems involve loss because the processes of identification of the 'meaning' of an entry are inadequate. When indexing is done by keywords alone the distortion can be large. In 'free-tests' retrieval methods, where the input is unaltered text (usually abstracts), the equivalent indexing processes are performed in the question at their input. Attempts have been made to remedy the defects by simple classificatory devices (links, roles, etc.) without much success. The more usual method has been to connect words by 'logic', almost always by the simplest form of Boolean algebra (the connectors 'and', 'or' and 'not'). Such logic suits the binary operations of a computer, but represents only a small part, and not even the most important part, of the logical processes which the human mind has been shown to use. Distortion of information is then inevitable, producing well known errors.[8]

Moreover, such processes of information transfer tend to hide the philosophical, cultural and subjective aspects of information and make it appear as though it were 'neutral', and therefore more relevant than it really is.

When the emphasis is on information and its provision, the context and complexity of the communication process is overlooked. The conventional image of communication, dominant in information science circles, is the one-way, purposive, vertical, top-down model; this is sender to provider orientated and looks at the whole process from the perspective of the message giver — raising questions of persuasiveness, effectiveness, conversion — rather than meeting basic needs.

A more sophisticated model of the communication process is provided by an old Sufi aphorism which asks: 'Is there a sound in the forest if a tree crashes down and no one is around to hear it?'. The right answer to this question is, of course, 'No.' The falling tree generates no noise unless it is perceived by someone. Perception is the main component of communication. What the aphorism is actually saying is that the field of experience, the world of discourse of sender and receiver must overlap before communication can take place.[9] When we examine communication from the point of view of perception, we come to three realizations:

1. We realise that it is the recipient who communicates. The originator of communication only utters. Unless there is someone who hears, there is no communication.
2. We know that we cannot perceive in single quanta, rather we always perceive in configurations: single events are always perceived as a part

of a totality. As such one cannot communicate a single word; the entire man comes with it.

3. We know that we can perceive only in terms of our experience. Beyond that there is no communication. Furthermore, we cannot perceive unless we also conceive. Also, we cannot form concepts unless we can perceive. To communicate a concept is impossible unless the recipient can perceive it, that is unless it is within his perception. Moreover, we perceive, as a rule, what we expect to perceive. We see largely what we expect to see, and we hear largely what we expect to hear. The unexpected is often overlooked: it is either not seen or ignored.

As such, communication makes demands on the recipient. It asks him to become involved; to do something, to become someone, to believe something. It appeals to motivation. If communication fits in with the hopes and aspirations, the ethics and values, the objectives and the purpose of the recipient, it is powerful. Communication will be ignored and even resisted if it goes against them. This is why western scientists and technologists have so much difficulty in communicating with Muslim scientists: the recipients unconsciously reject what is being communicated.

Communication, therefore, is a much more sophisticated process than a simple shuttle of information. There can be no communication without some involvement. While information can be transferred from 'us' to 'them', there can be no communication if this is how it is perceived. Communication can only occur from one member of 'us' to another. This means that true communication can only take place between individuals who share a single world-view. Thus communication of science within the Muslim world is more a function of how much scientific information is generated by Muslim scientists themselves than how much information is transferred from the industrialized countries. It means further that science and technology cannot be allowed to determine needs; rather, information and communication needs should be identified and evaluated from the specific values of self-reliance and community participation, social justice and cultural authenticity and then scientific and technological policy formulated to meet those needs.

Thus developing a communication system for Muslim scientists and intellectuals is very much an internal affair for the *ummah*. It involves overall emphasis on indigenous scientific and technological research within the framework of a basic needs strategy; scientific and technological cooperation between Muslim countries; and identification and evaluation of information needs within the overall development strategy.

Promoting Communication of Science and Technology

As a matter of absolute priority, Muslim countries have to evolve and promote the traditional sources of communication such as learned and scientific journals and set up small regional information networks designed specifically to bring together and promote the exchange of ideas between Muslim scientists and intellectuals.

There is an absolute dearth of scientific and learned journals in the Muslim world. It is necessary to establish a host of primary and secondary journals geared towards scientists and intellectuals serving the Muslim world. The journal is the prime and most common tool of intellectual communication. Western scientific journals, as is evident from the discussion above, do not serve the needs of Muslim scientists and scholars. Most widely known scientific journals are specifically aimed at the industrialized countries for this is where they have traditionally found their readership. Muslim scientists have difficulty in publishing in these journals for the following reasons:

1. Most journals specialize in fields which, with few exceptions, are outside the domains of scientists in the Muslim countries.
2. Even for journals which cover a number of scientific disciplines, such as *Nature* and *Science*, the problems of the Muslim countries are irrelevant and therefore not worthy of space.
3. In most journals it is necessary to pay, in hard currencies, for publications.

Thus, even if it was not necessary to develop an internal communication system for science and ideas within the Muslim world, there would be a strong case for Muslim countries to publish journals for local use as well as for the use by their scientific communities. Well refereed, high quality journals are needed within the Muslim world in all areas of science and learning, from anthropology to zoology. However, it is not necessary for all Muslim countries to publish journals in all fields. Those countries with a strong scientific and intellectual community in a particular discipline can undertake to publish a prime journal in that field on behalf of the *ummah*. However, what is necessary is for the journal to be of sufficiently high standard for scientists and scholars working in that field throughout the Muslim world to recognize it as *the* journal for the promotion and recognition of their work and ideas. A handful of such journals covering theoretical and practical sides of natural and social sciences as well as the humanities would greatly lift the morale of scientists and scholars and radically transform the quality and relevance of science and learning.

Along with primary journals, we also need a host of secondary and tertiary publications to ensure bibliographical control of these journals and increase the current awareness of Muslim scientists and scholars. Abstract, indexing and review journals and current awareness bulletins need to supplement the acutely needed primary journals in and for the Muslim countries.

The communication of science and ideas promoted by primary, secondary and tertiary journals will be enhanced by establishing a host of information networks which may be a small number of institutions working on similar problems. The purpose of such networks is to bring into direct contact, say, biologists in Malaysia working on water-borne diseases and researchers in Egypt working on bilharzia, scientists in Sudan tackling the problem of river blindness and so on. Nile basin countries can join their research institutions tackling bilharzia and set-up a bilharzia information network. Research communities working on similar problems need to be identified and communication channels between them developed and strengthened so that they can work as a network sharing ideas and experiences. Cohesiveness, efficiency and equitable sharing of resources and information are essential elements of such networks. Proper coordination and timely sharing of research results will ensure that solutions to complex problems are found in optimum time. Here again, Muslim countries which have strong research communities in particular fields need to take the lead in that field and establish a local information centre. Information scientists in that centre have to identify similar communities in other Muslim countries and turn the centre into a networking institution. Such institutions need not be big; nor do they need a great deal of resources. All they need is a micro-computer to develop their database of information, contacts and a small library to stock documents and journals relevant to their field.

Moreover, there are a number of information services that disseminate development information and encourage cooperation between developing countries which can be used as a catalyst for promoting communication of science between Muslim countries. Notable amongst these are UNISIST and DEVSIS.

UNISIST was originally conceived as a World Science Information System but it is now defined as the Programme of International Cooperation in Scientific and Technical Information. One of its five stated objectives is to provide assistance to the developing countries by helping them to develop minimum bases of scientific information and by developing pilot projects in cooperation with other UN agencies by establishing national agencies, developing well-equipped library and documentation services, and preparing for adaptation to computer retrieval systems by seeing that information activities and procedures accord with international standards.

DEVSIS, Development Service Information System, aims at treating the central economic and social questions of development, and DEVSIS will concentrate on the collection and retrieval of information that the developing countries generate in pursuit of their missions. An action-path scheme for DEVSIS has the following structure: finding the facts; assessing the trends; diagnosing the problems; identifying the needs; prescribing solutions; establishing policies; defining plans; devising projects; operating projects; assessing the impact of action; evaluating success or failure. DEVSIS collects information which has been generated in response to the requirements of one of these paths, as well as on the economic and social environment in which development takes place.

In using the services of UNISIST and DEVSIS an important point ought to be borne in mind. The global information structure is constructed in such a way that an agency, however well meaning, cannot really promote transfer of scientific and technological information *between* developing countries. Most development agencies, including UNISIST and other UN agencies, despite their efforts to the contrary end up promoting unidirectional transfer of information: from the developed to developing countries. As such the user countries have to try consciously to manipulate the system so that it brings Third World countries together and promotes technical cooperation between them, rather than simply becoming yet another tool of western domination. In the long run, the concept of self-reliance should force Muslim countries to develop such systems themselves and not rely on western or UN assistance for such projects. We shall return to this question in Chapter 9.

Only by shifting the emphasis from the transfer of information from the industrialized countries to communication of science within the *ummah* can Muslim countries cure the isolation and suffocation of their scientists and thinkers and make their work more relevant to the needs and requirements of Muslim societies and culture. Unless there is an adequate system for the communication of science within the Muslim world, along with an appropriate information structure, we cannot expect our scientists and technologists to fulfil the responsibility that we place on their shoulders.

Information Needs of Muslim Scholars

In contrast to scientists, Muslim scholars have access to very few organized national or international information services. This is despite the fact that in the last two decades their need of information has multiplied several hundredfold. The publication of books and articles on Islam and the Muslim world has increased exponentially both in the Muslim world and the West since the advent of the much trumpeted 'Islamic resurgence'. Moreover, entire new disciplines, such as Islamic economics and Islamic anthropology, have emerged in the last decade or so. There are few languages in the world in which writing on Islam is not produced. Bibliographical control of this ever increasing and linguistically diverse material is one of the major challenges facing the Muslim world today.

Traditionally, Muslim scholars have had only one major, widely available source of information: *Index Islamicus*. The *Index* is a catalogue of articles on Islamic subjects in periodicals and other collective publications and first appeared as a cumulative bibliography in 1958 when it covered the period 1906–55. Thereafter, it appeared in five-year supplements; and since 1977 it has been published as a quarterly with five-year cumulations. *Index Islamicus* has a strong religious slant (an estimated 62 per cent of its contents) and its coverage of important Muslim languages, such as Urdu, is negligible. There have been arguments and counter-arguments about the strong western bias of the *Index*. However, the issues have been settled by Abdus Sattar and Sajjad-ur-Rahman whose study of four major indexing services — *Index Islamicus, Humanities Index, Social Sciences Citation Index* and *Social Sciences Index* — showed that 38 per cent of sample literature was not covered by any of these services.[10] This is in addition to their almost total neglect of the vast, and rapidly rising, literature produced on Islam in the Muslim world.

Western attempts to bring literature on Islam and its world-view produced in the West and the Muslim world under adequate bibliographical control have a long history. The first bibliography on the subject dates back to 1799 when Christian F. Schnurer published *Bibliotheca Arabica: Actum Nunc Atque Integram*. Its second edition provided a classified bibliography with detailed annotations, of edited and translated Arabic-language books published in Europe during 1505–1810.

Bibliotheca Arabica was followed by Victor Chauvin's twelve-volume, *Bibliographie des Ouvrages Arabes ou Relatifs aux Arabes Publiés dans l'Europe Chrétienne de 1810 à 1885*. In 1887, *Orientalische Bibliographie* began to provide recurrent coverage of Islamic literature for the first time. It ceased publication in 1911. In the same year, Hartford Seminary's quarterly journal *Moslem World* (later changed to *Muslim World*) began to carry surveys of periodical literature as part of each issue. *Der Islam* followed the same practice for two decades (1913–33). Also during the early twentieth century, Giuseppe Gabriele's *Manuale di Bibliografia Musulmana* (1916) and Gustav Pfannmuller's *Handbuch der Islamliteratur* (1923) became important works in the field. From 1952 to 1973, the year of its demise, *International Bibliography for the History of Religions*, provided adequate coverage both to book and periodical literature on Islamic Studies. During the early forties, *Bibliotheca Orientalis* (1943 +) and the *Middle East Journal (1947 +)* were added to the growing list of recurrent bibliographical sources on Islam and the Muslim World. In 1974, *British Society for the Middle East Studies Bulletin* also began to provide bibliographical reports on a regular basis.

The first abstract journal in the field appeared in 1927. *Abstracta Islamica* began publication as a supplement to *Revue des Etudes Islamiques*. It remained the sole abstract journal in the field till 1976 when *Science of Religion: Abstracts and Index of Recent Articles*, which is supposed to replace the defunct *International Bibliography for the History of Religions*, began publication. The following year, *Bulletin Signalétique 527: Histoire et Sciences des Religion* began to provide abstracts of selected articles on Islam. *Middle East: Abstracts and Index* (1978) and *Mideast File* (1982) are new additions to western abstract and indexing journals of material on Islam and the Muslim world.

To point out that these journals and services are designed to cater for western scholarship, or that they have a strong western bias, or they ignore a large proportion of material published in the Muslim world, adds little to our knowledge. That western bibliographical tools should serve western interests seems obvious. However, that these tools also serve an ideological purpose is not widely recognized. Their undeclared objective is to preserve and dominate the intellectual space called Islam, the Middle East, the Muslim world. Elsewhere, in an analysis called *The Middle East: Abstracts and Index*, I have written:

> An abstract and index journal covering the Middle East which does not consider that the category 'Islam' deserves an individual and separate entry is clearly making an ideological statement. However, to make 'religion and philosophy', in other words, 'world-view', subservient to history, politics

and sociology and reduce it to an unimportant, tertiary category, is the height of Western arrogance. An average issue of *The Middle East* leaves no doubt in anyone's mind who controls the intellectual space called 'the Middle East' in various disciplines. For example, the September 1978 issue, chosen at random, devotes 37 pages of abstracts to Israel in comparison to 13, 8 and 3 to Egypt, Saudi Arabia and Jordon, respectively. Of the 350 journals covered, less than a dozen would classify as giving the Muslim or Arab viewpoints, while the vast majority represent Israeli, Zionist and American outlooks. The overall impression is that the Middle East itself is intellectually sterile; that the only thought worthy of consideration on the Middle East, in any recognized discipline, comes from the Western, including Israeli, literati. As such, *The Middle East* safeguards the intellectual space carved out by Western academic and journalistic circles. A 'scientific' study will simply give 'scientific' and 'objective' legitimacy to what *The Middle East* is designed to do: prove the intellectual superiority of the dominant culture.[11]

This objective is not limited to *The Middle East*: it is true of most bibliographical, abstract and indexing tools. It is also true of on-line data bases: a preliminary study of the coverage of Islamic literature by sixteen leading on-line data bases carried out by Yaghmai and his colleagues revealed that they cover 'primarily English language material produced in the United States, very little of which deals specifically with the cultural components of the Arab-Islamic world'. The situation here is a direct parallel to the transfer of scientific and technological information from the industrialized countries: in both cases, the overall effect is to induce further dependency and cultural imperialism in the Muslim countries.

Muslim scholars and journalists who use these tools suffer from two intrinsic diseases: as they do not see their own works indexed and abstracted in these journals they are led to believe that the quality of their own scholarship is somewhat inferior and the journals in which they publish are not important. They lack a real feeling for the thriving intellectual activity that is going on all around them. A whole new trend of Islamic thought, as exemplified in such new and emerging disciplines as Islamic economics, Islamic anthropology, Islamic futures, Islamic science and the study of Islamic movements, is not looked upon with favour by western academe and the editors of western journals. Thus a major proportion of contemporary Islamic scholarship, which is tackling the most pressing issues from the perspective of Islamic notions of self-reliance, social justice and cultural authenticity and which can contribute to the development of thought of young Muslim scholars, finds no place in western bibliographies, abstracts, indexes.

Muslim response to such blatant ideological manipulation has been, on the whole, quite encouraging. Muslim scholars are becoming aware of the limitations and bias of western bibliographical methods. Indeed, in certain new disciplines concrete and systematic attempts have been made to bring the growing literature under bibliographical control. In Islamic economics, for example, a number of bibliographies have appeared over the last few years, including the excellent literature survey by Nejatullah Siddiqui, *Muslim Economic Thinking*[12] and Muhammad Akram Khan's, *Islamic Economics — Annotated Sources in English and Urdu.*[13] For the study of Islamic movements, Asaf Hussain's *Islamic Movements in Egypt, Pakistan and Iran: An Annotated Bibliography*[14] is an indispensable tool. The history of Islamic science has been changed radically with the emergence of Faut Sezgin's *Geschichte des Arabischen Schrifttums* — eight out of twenty planned volumes have now been published — which contains over 1.5 million entries on Islamic scientific manuscripts covering the first four centuries of Islam.[15]

In more traditional areas, such as the study of the Qur'an and Hadith, bibliographical tools presenting the Muslim perspective are slowly becoming available. The monumental *World Bibliography of Translations of the Meanings of the Holy Qur'an — Printed Translations 1515–1980.*[16] prepared under the auspices of the Organization of Islamic Conference's International Research Centre for Islamic History, Art and Culture (IRCICA), constitutes the first major Muslim attempt to bring this vast, and vitally important, field under bibliographical control. Munawar Ahmad Anees and Alia Nasreen Athar's *Sira and Hadith Literature in Western Languages* does a similar job on the second fundamental source of Islamic law and thought. Indeed, Anees and Athar's bibliography goes straight into the area hitherto controlled and dominated by the orientalists, with a predictable response from the orientalist syndicate.[17].

Certain Muslim institutions have now started to produce subject bibliographies in areas relating to Islamic studies. The Islamic Documentation and Information Centre of Karachi University is publishing a whole series of subject bibliographies on topics such as literature on the Qur'an in English and doctoral dissertations on Islam. Extensive work on dissertations and theses produced in the Muslim world is being carried out at the King Abdul Aziz University in Jeddah, Saudi Arabia.

A number of serial publications devoted to bringing Muslim thought under bibliographical control have also appeared over the last decade. The serial of major importance amongst these is the Islamic Foundations' quarterly *Muslim World Book Review* which not only provides a critical perspective of new books on Islam and related themes published in the West and the Muslim world, but also regularly publishes subject bibliographies on contemporary Muslim thought. Recently, it has also started publishing a current awareness list. The quarterly *Information Bulletin* of the World Council of Islamic Studies is devoted to listing new publications in Arabic and English. Similar publications in Muslim languages include the quarterly *Alam al-Kutub* published from Riyadh and *Kitab Dergisi* which appears from Istanbul and the bi-monthly *Akhbar at-Turath* published by the Arab League Educational, Cultural and Scientific Organization's Institute for Arab Manuscripts in Kuwait.

All this is an indication of increasing Muslim awareness of the importance of information management and bibliographical control of the rapidly growing scholarship on Islam. However, these are only the first few, small, steps on a very long journey. While, out of necessity and a growing awareness of cultural and ideological bias, communication amongst Muslim scholars is increasing and they are assuming a more active part in bringing their own output under bibliographical control, certain specific steps need to be taken to consolidate the position and improve the overall situation. There is a need for specific serials such as *Current Contents of Muslim Journals* and *Islamic Abstracts*. Little improvement can be made without establishing annual national union lists of Muslim scholarship. A number of important data bases, not just on the Qur'an and Hadith — work on which has been started at Al-Azhar University in Cairo, King Saud University in Riyadh, and East–West University in Chicago — but also on such specific subjects as Islamic economics, history of Islamic science, Islamic art, museum holdings, cultural property, need to be set up. Moreover, all this information has to be coordinated and brought under the control of unified — not necessarily centralized — systems. There is a clear need for a clearing house of information on Islam and the Muslim world. But we shall leave the discussion on this and similar matters for Chapter 9.

To a very large extent, both improving the bibliographical control of Muslim material on Islam and Muslim societies and strengthening the communication of science within the Muslim world are dependent on the national bibliographical agencies and information systems in Muslim countries. Unfortunately, out of the forty-five member states of the Organization of Islamic Secretariat, only twenty-eight countries have national bibliographical agencies which bring out annual national bibliographies. Some of these countries, like Pakistan, remain in arrears for up to five years. Only Chad, Indonesia, Iraq, Kuwait and Malaysia publish their bibliographies quarterly; and only Egypt publishes a monthly national bibliography. While thirty-two countries have scientific and technological documentation centres, their activities are very limited and restricted, geared largely to promoting the transfer of information from industrialized countries. Without a basic national information infrastructure, it will not be easy for Muslim countries to set up much needed scientific information networks, data bases and develop bibliographical tools. It is to a discussion of evolving a modicum of national information infrastructures in Muslim countries that we turn next.

Notes

1. See my earlier books, *Science, Technology and Development in the Muslim World*, Croom Helm, London, 1977; and the 'Over-View' section of *Science and Technology in the Middle East*, Longman, London, 1982.
2. The classical description of scientific knowledge as private property is given by J.R. Ravetz, *Scientific Knowledge and Its Social Problems*, Oxford University Press, 1972.
3. UNESCO, *Science, Technology and Developing Countries*, Paris, 1977.
4. Colin Norman, *The God That Limps*, W.W. Norton, New York, 1981, p. 71.
5. UNESCO, Intergovernmental Conference on Scientific and Technological Information for Development, UNISIST II, Final Report, UNESCO, Paris, 1950, p. 20.
6. See Claude Alvares, 'The Dangerous, the Useless and the Needy', *Inquiry*, **3**(10) 26–33 (1986).
7. S. Salem, 'The Role of Information in Science and Technology Transfer in Arab Countries', *Journal of Information Science*, **2** 255–61 (1980).
8. J.E.L. Farradane, 'Information Science: Some Basic Problems', *Quest: Journal of the City University*, 26, Spring 1974.
9. The technocrat always fails to see the subtleties of traditional wisdom. Thus, J.E.L. Farradane in *The Information Scientist* (the predecessor of *Journal of Information Science*) 10(3) 91–101 (1976): 'We must not let ourselves be misled by the sort of quibble that suggests that a light or sound is not there if no one is there to see or hear it; this fallacy arises from the confusion caused by using the same word for physical light or sound wave as well as for the precept or concept engendered in the mind. We must always distinguish between the medium of communication and the mental interpretation of the recipient'. What word? Who is confused? What kind of mind would try to look for equations in an aphorism? See also the brilliant analysis of J.D. Halloran which puts crude technocrats in their place: 'Information and Communication: Information is the Answer, But What is the Question?', *Journal of Information Science*, **7** 159–67 (1983).
10 A. Sattar and Sajjad-ur-Rahman, 'Coverage of Islamic Literature in Selected Indexing Services', *International Library Review*, **17**(4) 357–70 (1985).
11. Ziauddin Sardar, 'Intellectual Space and Western Domination: Abstracts, Bibliographies and Current Awareness', *Muslim World Book Review*, **4**(2) 3–8 (1984).

12. M. Nejatullah Siddiqui, *Muslim Economic Thinking*, Islamic Foundation, Leicester, 1981.
13. Muhammad Akram Khan, *Islamic Economics — Annotated Sources in English and Urdu*, Islamic Foundation, Leicester, 1984.
14. Asaf Hussain's *Islamic Movements in Egypt, Pakistan and Iran: An Annotated Bibliography*, Mansell, London, 1983.
15. Faut Sezgin's, *Geschichte des Arabischen Schrifttums*, Brill, Leiden, 1974–82 (8 volumes published).
16. Ismet Binark and Halit Eren, *World Bibliography of Translations of the Meanings of the Holy Qur'an — Printed Translations 1515-1980*, IRCICA, Istanbul, 1986.
17. Munawar Ahmad Anees and Alia Nasreen Athar, *Sira and Hadith Literature in Western Languages*, Mansell, London, 1986.

8

Nations and States
Developing National Information Systems

The establishment and successful development of a system of communication of science within the *ummah* presupposes the existence of a viable information structure. While a few Muslim countries have certain types of national information services, national libraries and information centres catering for the scientific community, fully developed and integrated information infrastructures are conspicuously absent. An integrated information infrastructure — linking national libraries, computer-based data centres and archives with public and rural libraries, community information referral centres, reference and scientific information centres — is like the nervous system of a country. Knowledge flowing through this system is the vital life fluid which stimulates renewal and growth. Without it, Muslim countries are like a body without a nervous system: inert and static, unable to feel and adjust to change.

Without a developed and integrated information structure the smooth and efficient functioning of a modern government is impossible. All aspects of governmental activity in general, and development planning in particular, require information, though of different kinds. For example, goals cannot be outlined without some reference to the political system within which the planning process is set, and information on both the nature of goals and the mechanisms of the political system has to be disseminated throughout the community. It is the availability of a wide range of information on a variety of important subjects to a nation which makes it possible to comprehend the true magnitude of problems, set future goals, and choose wisely from a range of options. In choosing between alternative courses of action and policy, people require information on the possible outcome of this choice, as well as on techniques to achieve them and the assumptions behind them. Thus, information plays an important role in every aspect and stage of planning, administrative and policy work.[1]

Information becomes even more important when planning is seen as a continuous, holistic process. In general, planning in Muslim countries does not take the changing conditions of society into account; plans are made once and for all and some kind of process to implement them is instituted. However, as the plan is being implemented, society itself is changing which may render some aspects of the plan quite useless, or undermine the assumptions on which the planning process was based, or introduce situations where the implementation of the plan may, far from curing the problems it was originally designed for, actually aggravate them. Muslim decision-makers tend not to see planning as a dynamic process but as a static method of controlling the future development in the country. Moreover, they tend to concentrate on short-term, expedient plans rather than long-range, dynamic plans which accommodate change and development. They also seem to be unaware of the fact that one cannot make decisions for the present alone: most decisions commit us on a long-range basis.[2]

When these aspects of planning, including development planning, are considered, the true importance of information in sensing the pulse of a society and in structuring, implementing and communicating future plans comes into a sharper focus. A planning model describes the process by which plans are developed from impact data and from internal calculations. Information makes a theoretical as well as a practical contribution to the model. Information is the bond between relevant planning theory and relevant planning practice. Thus, any government which sets out to solve its national problems and improve the quality of life of its citizens, cannot hope to be successful without having a continuous supply of adequate information at its finger tips. And such a demand for appropriate information can be met only by developing a wide-ranging and thoroughly integrated information structure in the country.

We have discussed in previous chapters the importance of institutions which form the base of the national information infrastructure, such as public and rural libraries, scientific and scholarly information networks. These institutions serve as distributive networks for the dissemination of information to the appropriate segments of society. A fully-fledged information infrastructure also requires a number of national centralized institutions which serve as collectors of information. Collectively, both the distributive and centralized information agencies could be called the National Information System (NIS). As Wijasuriya points out, the NIS is a complex whole, with a number of sub-systems, and all 'the elements that constitute it should be organized or should function in proper relation to one another'.[3]

The centralized components of the NIS are:

1. A national library and documentation centre which serves as a deposit of all national publications and collects together, in one building, all documents which may be needed for indigenous research and development, scholarly and intellectual activities.
2. National specialized information centres for: science, technology and industry, medicine, agriculture, business and finance, law and education. Each of these vital sectors of economy and society must be served by a specialized information centre, equipped with appropriate technologies.
3. A national centre for information transfer (NCIT) to act as an information exchange, rather like a telephone exchange, linking scientists and scholars with similar interests to each other and promoting non-documentary channels of information transfer such as symposia, seminars and conferences.
4. A national standards institution to standardize the quantity, quality, pattern, methods and units of measurement in science and technology, industry and medicine, publications and information services as the accepted common minimum or example of standardization.

National Library and Documentation Centres (NLDC) are a major element in NIS. A NLDC is the centre of gravity for documentation in a country. It must therefore be in a position to make its services available to the entire nation. This may not be possible in many Muslim countries without a well-developed infrastructure. But it is necessary that the Centre should at least meet some of the national requirements of dissemination and information control.

More specifically the NLDCs must perform two roles crucial to the development function of information. Firstly, NLDC must collect together in one building all the documents which may be needed for the indigenous research and development activities. The use of the word 'all' needs a little explanation. Certainly documents originating locally must all be collected in the NLDC. Some countries will have institutions (national libraries, archives, etc.) which will have similar aims in relation to certain categories of documents. However, NLDC should concentrate on all areas and disciplines which are pertinent to local R and D efforts, as well as local material on social sciences and humanities. This collection is acquired and preserved for all persons who cannot conveniently meet their requirements elsewhere. The NLDC has a duty to acquire and preserve a nation's written heritage for posterity. Other roles are also added to the responsibilities of NLDC depending upon a number of factors, such as the government's view of NLDC, the size of the country, and its developmental stage. When considering documents of external origin 'all' acquires a limited meaning. Remembering that little over one per cent of the research carried out in the occident has any significance to the developing countries, NLDCs have to be selective in their collection of material. Preference should be given to documents originating in other developing countries, international agencies which involve themselves in development activities and those institutions in the occident that produce material of direct relevance to the developing countries such as the Science Policy Research Unit, the Institute of Development Studies of the University of Sussex, and the Intermediate Technology Group, to cite three British examples. The temptation for NLDC to collect material on all sorts of conspicuous areas of science and technology must be resisted. This will only generate 'noise' and create storage and handling problems.

Secondly, NLDC must take responsibility for international dissemination of documents originating within its national territory. This role is just as important as the first, being the most constructive an NLDC can make to the improvement of the international documentation of developing countries. Here too preference should be given to developing countries where documents could be disseminated on an exchange basis.

The second role of NLDCs demands more dedication than the first. While the first simply requires the NLDCs to act in a recipient capacity the second forces them to be outgoing and aware of what is going on in other developing countries. To achieve the first goal NLDCs need only traditional instruments of documentation. To achieve the second they will have to develop their own information delivery systems and acquire a high degree of documentary independence, thus enabling them to give full treatment to all their holdings. Within these two roles are a number of functions which have to be performed by NLDCs. They should:

1. Serve as copyright deposit centres.
2. Publish a national bibliography.
3. Serve as a national bibliographic centre.
4. Serve as a national reference and research library.
5. Work for compilation and publication of a Union catalogue.
6. Help in the development of inter-library loan programmes amongst various libraries in the country.
7. Devise and develop classification and cataloguing schemes to suit local needs and requirements.

Most developing countries either do not possess an NLDC or have a very poor institution performing this function.[4] Many factors are responsible for this situation. The main reasons are:

1. Lack of interest on the part of the governments of the Third World towards the development of NLDCs.
2. Ineffective professional organizations in the developing world.
3. Lack of a suitable authority to develop the NLDCs.
4. Absence of copyright and legal deposit provisions in many developing countries.
5. Lack of professional advice at all levels — planning, policy-making — and the resultant poor financing.
6. Lack of appropriate financial resources.

These problems are deeply rooted in the Third World. Their solutions cannot be partial, or palliative, but lie in the very fabric of developing societies.

Almost every Muslim country claims to have a national library. Indeed, some are over a hundred years old: the National Library of Algeria was established in 1835, the Egyptian National Library was established in 1870, the Al-Zahiriah National Library of Syria was founded in 1880 and the Bibliothèque Nationale of Tunisia was founded in 1885. But these national institutions do not perform the necessary functions of NLDC; they simply act as storehouses of books.[5]

A Specialized Information Centre (SIC) 'makes it its business to know everything that is published in a special field; it collects and reviews the data, and provides its subscribers with regularly issued compilations, critical reviews, specialized bibliographies and other such tools'.[6] In a developing country the function of SICs is to provide specialized information, without undue 'noise', in areas that enhance self-sufficiency, self-reliance and self-development. Some of the acutely needed SICs in

Muslim countries are: alternative energy sources, desalination, arid zone research, preventive and Islamic medicine, agriculture, mining and geological research, economic and industrial research, development and rural planning, information and library research, rural development, urbanization, educational research, forest research and mass communication.

Amongst the Muslim states, Malaysia has the most sophisticated and highly developed SICs. Although largely a post-war development, three of the largest SICs in Malaysia were established before 1930. The libraries at the Institute of Medical Research, Nuclear Research Institute and the Forest Research Institute established in 1901, 1925, and 1929, have given Malaysia a clear lead in these fields in the Third World.[7] Recently, however, Pakistan, Iran, Indonesia, Nigeria, Saudi Arabia and Turkey have also created SICs to meet the needs of local research and development activities.[8]

The problems associated with the development of SICs are common throughout the Muslim world. There are no agencies responsible for this aspect of information development. The library associations have not been able to formulate any policies as regards SICs. Neither have any standards for SIC been laid down. As such there is no guide on the basis of which research organizations or government agencies could develop SICs to meet their acute information needs. Every institution and organization works according to its own standards. Where a little development has taken place it is haphazard and most of the material remains unclassified due to the inability of the well-known classification schemes to meet the needs of SICs.

One particularly serious problem is the acquisition of material of foreign origin. There are few periodicals in the relevant fields but even those present serious problems: import restrictions even from other developing countries, lack of foreign exchange, customs regulations, postal formalities — all present hurdles that are seldom overcome. When these problems are compounded by the lack of trained manpower, we can see why SICs have not been able to gain a foothold in the developing world.

The existing SICs suffer from a number of defects. Very few Third World SICs have a provision for indexing periodicals or for providing and preparing special bibliographies for their clients. Translation facilities are almost unheard of. It is necessary for SICs in Muslim countries to be in touch with both their particular collection and the research scholars in that field, to know their needs and requirements and to interpret the Centres' services to them.

Many of the existing SICs in Muslim countries would benefit from the programme of the Industrial Information Section of the Industrial Services and Institutions Division, of UNIDO.[9] IIS offers advice and assistance to Third World countries for the establishment and management of national facilities for industrial information. This assistance includes not just organizational help but also the identification of the real needs for such information, the best ways and means to collect information and its dissemination to the potential users. Herbert Schwoeroel gives a list of areas and fields of information that are needed for positive decision-making in industrial enterprises:

1. Market information in the broadest possible sense: domestic and foreign markets, especially those of other developing countries; tariffs, taxes and other market restrictions, prices including prices of competitors, availability of transport and distribution facilities.
2. Information on industrial processes, equipment, appropriate technologies, appropriateness of technologies to local conditions, climate, labour, environment, prices, capacities, availability of spare parts, maintenance and repair facilities. This information is essential for the purchase and development of appropriate technology and equipment.
3. Information on raw materials and semi-finished goods, full exploration of local raw materials etc.
4. Infrastructural information, availability and supply cost of energy, water, transportation, quality of electric current as a pre-condition for the use of certain types of machinery, labour situation, training opportunities, wages, social insurances, availability of qualified managerial and administrative staff.
5. Information on industrial environment, services, R and D facilities, industrial legislation including patents, trade marks, designs and licensing, industrial chambers and associations, inquiry and extension services, export promotion etc.

Similar lists can be drawn for specialized information for agriculture, development, educational development, legal and political information and other areas and fields of particular concern to developing countries.

As discussed in Chapter 7, communication between scientists and scholars within a single Muslim country and within the Muslim world as a whole, is a serious problem. This is where National Centres for Information Transfer come in. Their purpose is to link scientists and scholars with the information they desire or scientists and scholars with similar interests, and promote documentary as well as non-documentary channels of information transfer such as symposia, seminars, and conferences. Also NCIT perform the function of informing users of current research and development efforts pertinent to their interests and guiding the national scientific community in its communication endeavours with scientific communities of other developing countries. The latter function is performed more specifically via:

1. A Current Awareness Service through which contents of current periodicals, journals and other documents taken in the library and information network of the country is circulated at regular intervals on a subscription basis to those interested. Usually this is achieved by publication of monthly current awareness bulletins in various fields; the bulletins may in some cases contain abstracts of cited references.
2. Selective Dissemination of Information (SDI) through which selected items are provided to scientists and scholars by scanning current R and D literature and matching them against recorded profiles of individuals and groups. The SDI services are usually computerized but in developing countries there is no essential reason why this should be so.
3. Information Retrieval Service through which references specified by author or subject are researched and supplied in the form of a list of references, abstracts, microform or hardcopy, as desired. For comprehensive services, especially in certain currently fashionable fields, it is necessary to computerize this service.

Certain countries operate useful and reasonably well-known NCITs. Those of Turkey (TURDOC), Pakistan (PASTIC, formerly PANSDOC) and Saudi Arabia (SANCST) are well known. However, the trend has to be spread, and the services of the existing centres must be improved considerably.

While the importance of NLDC, SIC and NCIT are readily recognized, the role played by the national standards institution is not fully appreciated. Standardization is defined as the setting up, by authority or common consent, of a quantity, quality, pattern, method, or unit of measurement for adoption as a common minimum or as an example of unitation. Standardization is of crucial interest to developing countries for at least three basic reasons. Firstly, internationally accepted standards promote export by providing certain access to the markets of the developed countries. Secondly, imported machinery, equipment and material can be ordered to a particular specification, thus saving costs, simplifying maintenance and purchase of spare parts as well as reducing stocks of spare parts. Thirdly, standardizing indigenous technology at an accepted level improves local products and technological efforts.

The function of a National Standards Institution is to specify levels of standards — these relate to dimensions, quality, performance, methods of test and control, codes of practice, technical terms and symbols etc. — and to keep some kind of check to ensure that they are being met.

A number of Muslim countries have well-established Standards Institutions: those in Malaysia, Iran, Turkey, Saudi Arabia and Indonesia are fully operational. Other Muslim countries need to emulate them.[10]

The basic requirements for setting up and evolving national information systems are common to all Muslim countries. At least eight essential features can be identified:

1. Administrative and organizational requirements: a central administration and policy-setting organization is required to coordinate and implement overall national policy for information. Also comparable cost data must be acquired and analysed and regular reviews made of the various sub-systems of the NIS. Overall planning and coordination is necessary to achieve long-range goals of NIS. Included in this requirement is the need to provide for coordination of the development of certain facilities, including central computer stores and microfilm reproduction and storage centres.

2. User orientated requirements: the system must be designed to handle an increasing number of requirements and a wide range of users including scientists, technologists, scholars, academics, industrialists, government administrators, policy-makers, managers and legislators. The system should provide a wide range of services to its users.

3. Requirements for the internal operation of the system: the system should contain at least one reproducible, significant copy — according to the criteria outlined above — of domestic and foreign documents and at the same time should be able to minimize duplication of acquisition. There must be regular reviews of the status of the document collection of the system and each of the sub-systems must have knowledge of the principle subject content sufficient to isolate desired documents in the systems.

   The redundancy in the system should be minimal and criteria and methods should be developed to keep redundancy in check. This would require consideration of: overlaps in collections; duplication of indexes, abstracts, and translation of the same document; duplication of loans, reproduction and reference services; on-going studies and reviews of duplication services. Concerning the processing manipulation of information, it is necessary to develop standards and compatibility of the various parts.

4. Requirements regarding reproduction and representation of documents: these requirements are concerned with the capacity of the system to handle increases in the number of documents and maintain control over their dissemination. The system should encourage the improvement of document quality and the reduction of the volume of documents by efficient use of critical review, technical evaluation, retiring of unused or infrequently used material and bibliographical control of collections. This implies:

   a) Improved acquisition policies including the coordination of acquisitions among the sub-systems of the system;
   b) The development of methods of screening documents by critical reviews;
   c) There is a need for providing for the archival function i.e., the function of ensuring the permanent retention of at least one accessible copy of each document entering the system;
   d) There is a requirement for the development of explicit policies on the retiring of documents from functional collections.

5. Requirements of dissemination and special services: the system must continually re-evaluate its dissemination techniques. These include:

   a) Providing for appropriate channels and mechanisms for the storing and dissemination of documents.
   b) Responsibility for the capability of the system to provide a hard copy, microform or computer disc of each document.
   c) Provision of efficient and timely distribution of documents.
   d) Establishing criteria and guidelines concerning application of active dissemination techniques.
   e) The system should provide for the dissemination of oral and other informal modes of information transfer.

6. System evaluation requirement: the system should be re-evaluated periodically and adjusted to meet the demands of changing circumstances. However, changes and improvements in the system should be evolved in a manner which does the least possible disruption to the system. It should be designed to adjust effortlessly to changing requirements.

7. Education and training requirements: the healthy growth of any system demands that there is always sufficient and skilled manpower

to operate it. This includes professionals such as information scientists, librarians, reprographic experts, computer scientists, systems analysts and clerical personnel. This requires that the system:

a) Gives examples and suggestions for curricula in universities and colleges.
b) Sets standards for professional qualifications and provides in-service and on-the-job training.
c) Provides support, consultancy and subsidies to appropriate institutions.
d) Helps specify performance standards for various tasks to be performed.

8. R and D requirements. For the system to develop and thrive, there is need for a coordinated programme of research and development on the system as a whole and on its various sub-systems.

These are the essential requirements of any National Information System. It is evident that there can be no single plan or structure that can be used as a typical pattern for all Muslim countries. The infrastructures and styles of government in the Muslim world differ widely; and each NIS will be as different as the people of various countries. The individual systems have to be closely adapted and must conform with the infrastructure and administration of Muslim countries.

However, any system proposed must be evolutionary in character in the sense that it must start and develop from the existing systems — libraries, archives, information centres, documentation centres — and evolve in a form which is consistent with an overall plan. The important point is that the existing information agencies, often fragmented and isolated, must be combined on the basis of a consistent, long-range plan. The new institutions must interact and interlink the existing institutions to form a unified, holistic system.

The NIS and its sub-systems should not be conceived in terms of a primitive model which perceives them as linear systems receiving raw data and instructions, processing data according to given instruction, and feeding out the results. This model in terms of input and output processes is suitable only for the simplest information processing systems where the entire input comes at the same time. This happens only rarely. It would happen if NIS were being set up from scratch, without any existing information agencies in the country and when it was designed to solve all problems at one stroke. More commonly, the NIS needs data that has been collected, analysed and processed at a prior period in existing information agencies. The data handling capability of the NIS therefore has to be flexible so that the processing activity has access to both the current data as well as the data gathered and stored previously. The design of NIS involves a complex series of choices in which no particular decision is independent of any other decision which has already been made or which is to be made.

The basic aim of any national information system should be the development of the ability to provide scientists, technologists, sholars, professionals, students and other qualified individuals with at least one accessible copy — that is, a copy or a reproduction which could be made available to the user in a reasonable time — of each *significant* publication of the world-wide literature. Here the notion of significant is very important: considering that over 97 per cent of the information output of the world has no significance for Muslim countries, as discussed in Chapter 4, the national information system should not overload itself with the flood of information coming from the North. The relevance of documents to national users can be determined only by research into the needs of local user groups, a rationalized policy of accession and wise judgement. The primary responsibilities of each sub-system of the NIS should be clearly and precisely defined so that the sub-systems do not duplicate services or attempt to serve one user group at the expense of another. Moreover, it should avoid the indiscriminate proliferation of services.

An NIS should be gradually evolved and not established in one giant leap. It is tempting to think in terms of machines, automation and computers which can solve all national information problems instantly. But as we discussed in Chapter 2, information technologies are a double-edged sword which need to be handled with caution and wisdom. Information technologies should not be introduced indiscriminately without assessing the real need for them. In most cases, the traditional methods of acquiring and disseminating information would be more than adequate for most Muslim countries. Automation and computerization do not always improve the performance of an information system; indeed, they may generate a host of new problems much more complex and difficult to solve. As most of the international communication of the NIS would be with other Muslim and developing countries, where the bulk of the information for a country's national needs would be found, the decision not to computerize may be more beneficial: no one ever sent manuals on water-management in rural areas or alternative health-care through an information network. Computerizing a national library does not necessarily improve its performance. Simply putting the catalogue on a computer file and mechanizing the loan system does not answer the basic systems questions about the users of the library and their needs. However, in certain specialized information agencies of the sub-systems of the NIS, where information is required in terms of brief, discrete data, small computerized systems may be beneficial. The important point is that information technologies are not a panacea for everything; just as for other technologies, their usefulness too must be examined.

The development of national information systems has been hampered in Muslim countries by a deliberate policy of ignoring the importance of information: the dominant political elite feel threatened by the whole idea of developing an information infrastructure and permitting free flow of information. Libraries and information centres are seen in a political context as agents of change. But to ignore the importance of information in modern society is not only shortsighted, it can also cause catastrophic and irreparable damage to Muslim societies. Governments should accept the fact that information is a major national resource and the development of an infrastructure would lay the foundation for healthy growth and development.

It is largely due to government policies of ignoring the importance of information that the efforts of library associations and societies to obtain a high priority for NIS in the overall national development programmes have failed over the past two decades. However, minor successes have been achieved in Saudi Arabia, Pakistan, Turkey and Nigeria. Undoubtedly, the most successful effort has been made in Malaysia; the National Library Act of Malaysia is considered to be a milestone for library development in the Muslim world. Other Muslim countries would do well to follow in their footsteps. The main features of the Malaysian Library Act are contained in Part II (3) which considered that the functions of the National Library should be to:

1. Provide leadership and promote cooperation in library affairs in Malaysia.
2. Assist the government in the promotion of the learning, use and advancement of the national language.
3. Support research and inquiry on a national scale.
4. Provide facilities for the enlightenment, enjoyment and community life of the people.
5. Contribute to the development of cultural relations with the people of other countries.
6. Provide or promote such other services or activities in relation to library matters as the Ministry may direct.

These are indeed enlightened and worthwhile objectives. But this achievement, only the first step towards the evolution of a comprehensive information infrastructure in the country, was possible in Malaysia where a proper machinery for policy-making, planning and execution, composed of qualified and experienced persons has successfully evolved. Other Muslim countries have to evolve such a machinery. This will involve setting up:

1. A policy council for NIS headed by the Minister of Information.
2. Setting up of an appropriate body in the Ministry of Planning to translate national policies into operational plans and to incorporate such plans into national development plans.
3. A secretariat for NIS in the Ministry of Education at central and regional levels to work out programmes for the implementation of the plans.
4. Library and information boards and committees at regional and provincial levels to execute the programme.
5. And an inspectorate for the sub-systems of the NIS in the Ministry of Education to ensure the proper execution and implementation of the programme.

The establishment of NIS and evolution of an integrated information infrastructure is one of the major challenges facing Muslim countries in the information age. Some resources for meeting this challenge already exist; others need to be developed. If Muslim countries fail to meet this challenge, they will pave the way for the onset of a new, more sophisticated and powerful age of colonialism.

Notes

1. For the relationship between information and decision-making, see the interesting discussion of Robert F. Barnes, 'Information and Decision', in *Perspectives in Information Science*, Anthony Debons and William J. Cameron (eds.), Leyden, Noordhoff, 1975, pp. 105–17.
2. For an alternative view of how information and planning can be used to reconstruct Muslim civilisation, see Ziauddin Sardar, *The Future of Muslim Civilisation*, 2nd rev. ed., London, Mansell, 1987.
3. D.E.K. Wijasuriya, 'The Development of National Information Systems', *Journal of Information Science*, **1**(1):27–34, (1979).
4. A.M. Abdul Haq and Mohammed M. Aman, *Librarianship and the Third World: An Annotated Bibliography of Selected Literature on Developing Nations, 1960–1975*, New York, Garland, 1977.
5. Sajjad ur Rahman, 'Databases and Networks: Present Status and Prospects

in the Muslim World', paper presented at the second COMLIS meeting, Malaysia, 20–22 October, 1986.

6. From the Weinberg Report, *Science, Government and Information*, GPO, Washington, 1963, quoted by J. Harvey, *Specialist Information Centres*, Bingley, London, 1976, p. 13.

7. See D.E.K. Wijasuriya *et al.*, *The Barefoot Librarian*, Bingley, London, 1975, for the development of librarianship in Southeast Asia in general and Malaysia in particular.

8. See S.J. Haider, 'Science-Technology Libraries in Pakistan', *Special Libraries* 65:474–78 (1974); K. Kaser *et al.*, *Library Development in Eight Asian Countries*, Metuchen, N.J., 1969; Pui-Huen, P. Lim *et al.*, *Proceedings of the First Conference of the Southeast Asian Libraries*, Singapore, 1972; and CENTO, *Regional Documentation Centres Conference*, 29 April–1 May 1974, CENTO Scientific Programme Report No. 12, 1975.

9. *Vide* H. Schwoeroel, 'Industrial Information: a guide to better understanding and indications of how to use assistance and services offered by UNIDO in introducing information as an instrument for industrialisation', in *Information System Design and Socio-Economic Development*, FID, The Hague, 1976.

10. See *Technology for Development through Standardization*, DIN Deutsches Institut fur Normung e.V., Berlin; prepared on the occasion of the United Nations Conference on Science and Technology for Development, 1979.

9

Power and Control

Co-operating for Information

The basic issues of access to information are issues of power and control. As information acquires the role of the chief raw material and the principal product, the distribution of information goods and services can be expected to be one of the basic factors shaping the power structure of the world in coming decades. Quincy Rogers' warning of ten years ago is now becoming a reality:

> Access to knowledge and information and to the channels through which it is conveyed will be important for a 'piece of the action' in the information age, both on the domestic scene and internationally. Major questions are now being asked: Who shall have access? For what purpose? What will be the procedure for granting or denying access? What are the costs involved and how are they to be allocated? As a logical result of the post-industrial society, postulated by Bell and others, these types of problems can be anticipated. But such logic is not the only clue. Struggles over access to information sources which government(s) is (are) already experiencing permeate many of the most valuable issues of our time. These controversies are being labelled by such terms as 'privacy', 'freedom of information', 'sunshine', and 'government secrecy', but their meaning is found in the concept of access. And as access becomes more central to the progress of our society then the ferocity of such clashes may well intensify.[1]

From the perspective of the Muslim world, information could well develop on the same lines as technology transfer and foreign aid. Whereas we now experience technological and aid dependency, a decade or so from today we may also experience information dependency. But information dependency would have many new and frightening dimensions: it would generate a form of colonialism unknown in human history.[2]

The demands of Islamic concepts which have shaped our inquiry so far — *tawheed, adl, hikma, shura, ijma,* and *ummah* — do not stop at the development of information infrastructure and institutions within national boundaries but go on to embrace the Muslim world as a whole. Dealing with the challenges of the information age requires a depth of understanding and ability to work in integrated and cooperative modes which the Muslim *ummah* has not achieved thus far. However, cooperation and integration in issues of information are not just demands of the values that we profess; they are imperative for the integrity and survival of Muslim people and culture.

What specific justifications are there for Muslim countries to cooperate? Sajjad ur Rahman argues that there are at least three reasons why it is essential for Muslim countries to share their resources in setting up joint information networks.

Firstly, the Muslim world is tied together with some infallible bonds of faith and creed, cultural heritage, civilizational development, and similarities in the socio-politico-economic structures of their societies. The Muslim world stretches in a wide area from north to south and from east to west on the globe with a noticeable diversity of languages, cultures, political structures, and economic status. However, natural affinity and harmony in some regional blocs make them vital strategic units to be studied with a pointed interest. Within the Arab world three regional affinities emerge, namely the Gulf countries, the Mediterranean tract, and the North African nations. Eastern and central African Muslim nations make another integrated unit. On the other end of the Middle east, Turkey, Iran and Pakistan present an opportunity for deepening relations in all spheres of societal development. Farther in the Far East, Malaysia and Indonesia have much in common to share with each other. This description may sound over simplistic, but the intent is to point out that within the Muslim world some viable socio-geographic entities possess innate linkups. This makes them natural candidates for any activity of resource sharing and networking. Secondly, Muslim countries form a bloc within the community of developing nations which has common concerns, problems, and challenges in their development programs. A focused examination of their situation elicit useful perspectives relevant to their development. Thirdly, there are definite areas of resource sharing which are unique prerogatives of the Muslim world. The resources of Islamic heritage and civilization originated in these lands, but they are desperately dispersed, without much help to trace them for researchers. Likewise, study and research in Islamic studies, Islamic law and jurisprudence, and other theological aspects of Islam demand a more coherent and integrated approach, both for the collection and organization of intellectual resources and for the delivery of information or documents.[3]

In addition, there are four other reasons for cooperation:

1. To improve the coverage and timeliness of information transfer by assessing material at or near its source.
2. Pooling valuable resoures to avoid unnecessary duplication of skills and material.
3. To benefit from the use of local linguistic skills for transforming document description into the languages of the system.
4. To maximize the use of available information resources, subject specialists and other skills.

There are some outstanding problems that can be solved only through cooperation: the difficulties produced by the increasing volume of world scientific and technical literature; faulty distribution practices; understocked and understaffed libraries; difficulty of systems to adjust to change; the lack of compatibility among information systems, and the lack of adequate and appropriate information infrastructure in many Muslim countries.

In response to these problems and pressures, cooperation may take many forms: from bilateral agreements to multi-national conventions; from informal exchange of documents, programmes, data bases, and personnel to international studies, seminars and conferences convened by Muslim governments and/or Muslim international organizations; from plans to set up regional and international networks and information systems to a whole kaleidoscope of activities which can be undertaken to promote cooperation and integration.

The eighties have seen some positive developments which indicate that cooperation is becoming a reality in the Muslim world. There has been, for example, the remarkable progress in setting up data communication services in the Middle East. The emergence of Gulfnet is one indication of this: a computer-to-computer network, it links eight academic and research institutions in the Gulf region: Umm al-Qura University, Makkah; King Abdul Aziz University, Jeddah; King Saud University, Riyadh; The Institute of Public Administration, Riyadh; King Abdul Aziz City for Science and Technology, Riyadh; King Faisal University, Dammam; University of Petroleum and Minerals, Dharan and The Kuwait Institute for Scientific Research, Kuwait.[4] In addition, an Arab Information Systems Network (ARISNET) is being established by the Arab League Documentation Centre (ALDOC). ARISNET will consist of three sub-systems: national information networks will cover development related information about the Arab world; sectoral networks will be devoted to information on priority sectors of Arab development; and mission-orientated networks will cover selected areas of concern to the Arab region on issues such as food, environment, health and population. The coordination of ARISNET throughout the Arab region will be achieved through a computerized network that will have database access and exchange possibilities with participating information centres. As a telecommunication-based network, which will utilize satellites, ARISNET will cater for two-way data transmission, on-line access, as well as the conventional means of information exchange such as telephone and telex.[5] Besides ARISNET, the Islamic Foundation for Science and Technology for Development is setting up a number of specialized networks on space science, renewable energy sources, ocean science, tropical medicine, bio-technology and bio-engineering and water resources.[6]

While these new networks will fill acute gaps in the provision of information in the Muslim world, it is, however, still necessary to establish two types of information services that link entities of the entire Muslim world: an International Muslim Information Network (IMIN) and an Islamic Reference and Information Service (IRIS).[7] IMIN should be a network serving the scientific and technological needs of the Muslim world, while IRIS should be an international agency and clearing house serving specifically the needs of a growing number of scholars and researchers working on the 'Islamization' of various disciplines. These information agencies should be conceived as civilizational institutions, linking and integrating the *ummah* and paving the way for its re-emergence as a dynamic and thriving contemporary civilization. We shall discuss the function and design of IMIN and IRIS in an outline form.

The objectives of IMIN will be to provide a network for making available existing and planned information sources for the benefits of the users and researchers throughout the Muslim world. This will involve:

1. Setting up of national information systems in all Muslim countries as discussed in Chapter 5.
2. The coordination of information activities throughout the Muslim world to avoid duplication.
3. The cooperative establishment of new information systems and scientific information networks as discussed in Chapter 4.
4. The provision of appropriate facilities throughout the Muslim world for communication and reprocessing of information.
5. The cooperative utilization of the information resources of the industrialized states by Muslim countries.

The essential function of IMIN would be to provide a medium for access to and exchange of information relating largely to science, technology, medicine, industry and agriculture as well as business and finance. The network would store information generated in the Muslim world, but would also provide a means of access to relevant scientific and technical information generated in the industrialized countries and would be capable of connecting with other networks. It should provide the following services:

1. The network should be able to transmit data to any major Muslim city for retrospective searches. Furthermore, it should be possible for the searchers, if they so wish, to send the results of their search to another location in the Muslim world.
2. The network should be able to make Selective Dissemination of Information (SDI) to researchers in all Muslim countries with profiles stored in the system.
3. The network should be able to take on the function of location and acquisition of documents and on-line cataloguing.
4. The network should be able to provide assistance in locating the data base most appropriate for the needs of individual users. In other words, it should be able to fulfil a referral function in guiding enquiries to the most relevant data bases.
5. Finally, the network should be able to gather statistics of its usage and performance which will be needed for the identification of problem areas (eg. frequency of breakdown), overload conditions, user behaviour etc., and for the purpose of network management and control.

To meet the above requirements and needs IMIN has to be a highly sophisticated multi-national, multi-disciplinary and multi-lingual network. This is not as tall an order as it appears at first sight. However, the design of IMIN will be a complex task and there will be considerable problems. Table 9.1 lists some of the problems the multi-national, multi-disciplinary and multi-lingual character of IMIN would generate.

There are two possible computer-based solutions to these constraints: a centralized or a distributed system. A centralized system may be centralized physically, that is all hardware and data bases are in one location together with the personnel, systems development, maintenance, administration etc. Alternatively, it may be centralized logically, that is, all data is stored on a single data base. A distributed system may be allocated in terms of separate data bases and processing hardware, or it may have logical form despite wide physical distribution — it could even be

Table 9.1   Problems arising from the multinational, multi-disciplinary and multi-lingual character of the International Muslim Information Network

---

Problems arising from the multinational character of IMIN

1. POLITICAL	Who has what share? Who pays? Where is it centred?	
2. LEGAL	Copyright. Private information (commercial and security). Ownership. Post Office payments.	
3. ECONOMIC	Payments for storing, retrieving, updating and maintenance. Capital expenses. Exchange rates. National use/private use. Payments pro-rata to what use, GNP number of users, etc.?	
4. PERSONNEL	Who needs it? How many of each? Employment of 'aliens'. Salary scales.	
5. TECHNICAL	What hardware/software? Transmission lines.	

Problems arising out of multi-disciplinary character of IMIN

1. POLITICAL	Whose data do we choose? In which order do we take them? How many similar ones or combined ones?	
2. ECONOMIC	Different use of subject data bases. Charges and payments.	
3. PERSONNEL	Communication of subject specialists within disciplines, across disciplines.	
4. TECHNICAL	Required different formats. Query language(s). Combining for interdisciplinary areas.	

Problems arising out of multi-lingual character of IMIN

1. POLITICAL	Language of documentation (English? Turkish? Malay?).	
2. LEGAL	Contracts.	
3. ECONOMIC	Languages for output.	
4. PERSONNEL	Multi-lingual/common language.	
5. COMMAND LANGUAGE	Translated on-line/printout.	

logically part of the same file. In such systems, distribution obviously extends to all the required hardware, personnel, functions, buildings. A few compromises are possible.

In terms of data bases, there are two possible approaches; centralized data base or distributed data base. Table 9.2 lists the pros and cons of both alternatives. Of course, the lists assume the worst problems. Wise choice of system, implementation, staff, or whatever, could easily negate the disadvantages and enhance the advantages.

For a centralized system the choice of hardware is not vital given good time-sharing, tele-processing and sufficient power. Availability of large desk store is a consideration. However, choice of data base maintenance is vital. The prime requirements are information retrieval capability and availability of data structure to handle (possibly) variable formats and relations. Site location is vital for telecommunications. For a variable dependable network, hardware service is naturally the most important factor. For a distributed system, the choice of hardware must be coordinated (at least) for technical compatibility. Personnel organization has to be handled skilfully to reduce development problems. Careful systems communication and data base(s) design can result in a properly integrated, efficient system with hardware that is unusually reliable. System maintenance is much simpler than is the case with the centralized system, but data control is more difficult.

The basic trade-off is hardware cost versus residence, and data control versus flexibility.

In the choice between a centralized or a distributed system the essence of the matter is not to hold all the information in one place but to hold information on information. The major decisions faced by IMIN are all political: site, location, funding, communication system etc. Indeed the basic choice between a centralized system or a distributed system can only be made by political criteria. As such, IMIN can link the major cities of the Muslim world and bring them closer towards cooperation and integration only if Muslim countries realize its importance and are willing to put aside some of their political differences.

While IMIN, of necessity, involves cooperation between Muslim governments IRIS would function better on the level of international organization. Traditionally, 'Islamic studies' have suffered from a lack of appropriate bibliographical control and proper dissemination. For example, there is no such thing as *Islamic Abstracts* which digests the output of Muslim scholars. However, what was normally classified as 'Islamic studies' is now going through a profound change: there is a proliferation of thought and activity designed to discover Islamic alternatives

Table 9.2 Advantages and disadvantages of centralized and distributed data bases

A centralized data base

	Advantages	Disadvantages
POLITICAL	Administration	Where? Who is in charge? Funding?
ECONOMIC	Single hardware Supplier Bulk purchase Centralized charging Reduced development time Better maintenance Site expenditure Telephone communications	Collecting of payments Selling Telephone communications
PERSONNEL	Less necessary Better selection On-site terminal possible	Relocation
TECHNICAL	Data integrity Data security Telecommunications design Updating Maintenance Systems support Command/enquiry Language	Hardware reliability Cumbersome data formats

A distributed data base

	Advantages	Disadvantages
POLITICAL	Siting of hardware	Administration? Who is in charge? Funding?
ECONOMIC	Sales Local charges/collection Telephone communication	Number of suppliers Transfer of costs Development duplication Development incompatibility Hardware maintenance System support Sites Telephone communication
PERSONNEL	Employed locally	Lots
TECHNICAL	Specialized formats Hardware duplication Local update Data security	Command/enquiry Language Telecommunications design Remote update Data integrity Maintenance/support

to almost every discipline. Thus, over the last two decades, an entirely new discipline, Islamic economics, has emerged: the literature, covering both theoretical and experimental aspects, is vast and growing exponentially. Similarly, a number of new disciplines — from Islamic anthropology to Islamic science, political theory, environmental theory, and Islamic futures — are struggling to be born. These new and vital disciplines are laying the intellectual foundation for the reconstruction of Muslim civilization. Unfortunately, researchers in these rapidly growing disciplines tend to work in isolation. For example, those working in Islamic economics seldom see the material produced by those working to establish an Islamic theory of environment, or trying to shape thought and ideas on the future of Muslim civilization. Because Islam encompasses an integrated and holistic world-view, the problems in different Islamic disciplines often have similar solutions. Thus if individual researchers and thinkers working on these new areas had access to the work of others, they would not only benefit greatly but would be able to produce more integrated and viable solutions. The objective of IRIS would be to provide a comprehensive information service both in the emerging new disciplines as well as in the traditional areas of Islamic studies. More specifically this would involve:

1. Monitoring the entire range of literature covering traditional Islamic studies and the emerging new disciplines.
2. Publishing a range of secondary sources: indexes, abstract journals, bulletins on issues indicating current awareness and bibliographies.
3. Publishing important works of reference such as encyclopaedias, dictionaries, yearbooks, guides, who's whos.
4. Providing a service for selective dissemination of information.
5. Establishing minimum standards for handling information as well as for the design and production of Muslim periodicals.
6. Promoting and encouraging the production of learned serials and community periodicals and acting as a clearing house for all Muslim publications.
7. Publishing Muslim sources of information and services and helping in the training of users to use effectively the available resources.
8. Collecting statistics and other data relevant to the needs of Muslim scholars, thinkers, intellectuals and journalists.

While it would require the support of international organizations to perform its function, IRIS should be established as an independent agency. An organization such as the Congress of Muslim Librarians and

Information Scientists would be an ideal institution for undertaking the responsibility of establishing IRIS. The manpower resources needed for an institution like IRIS are presented in Table 9.3

Table 9.3   Staffing of Islamic Reference and Information Services

DIRECTORATE	1 Director
	2 Associate Directors
	2 Staff Assistants
	3 Assistants
PUBLIC RELATIONS DEPARTMENT	2 Information Scientists
	2 Technical Writers
	2 Public Relations Specialists
	5 Assistants
ADMINISTRATION DEPARTMENT	3 Administrators
	2 Legal Counsel
	5 Accountants
	3 Facilities Engineers
	17 Assistants
SECONDARY SOURCES DEPARTMENT	7 Abstractors
	3 Indexers
	2 Bibliographers
	5 Scholars of Islam
	20 Assistants
REFERENCE DEPARTMENT	15 Scholars of Islam
	3 Librarians
	2 Editors
	20 Assistants
RESEARCH AND DEVELOPMENT TRANSLATION DEPARTMENT	7 Translators
	2 Information Scientists
	2 Information Planners
	3 Statisticians
	15 Assistants
DISSEMINATION AND USER ENQUIRIES DEPARTMENT	3 Information Scientists
	2 Librarians
	20 Assistants
PUBLICATION DEPARTMENT	1 Publisher and Senior Editor
	3 Editors
	2 Assistant Editors
	4 Design and Layout Experts
	20 Assistants
TOTAL	70 Professional Staff
	20 Scholars of Islam
	120 Support Staff

There are a number of possible placements for the agency. We would suggest, however, that the choice of a home for IRIS should be made on the basis of ease of communication. The city chosen to be the head-quarters of IRIS must have a well developed communication structure, postal services, telephones, transportation. It would be an advantage to place IRIS near an international airport so that the staff and visitors to the agency have easy access to the major cities of the Muslim world. The financial cost of running an agency like IRIS would be insignificant compared with the gain it would produce for the *ummah*, The only really astonishing thing about this proposal is that an agency like IRIS is not already functioning in the Muslim World.

Notes

1. Quincy Rogers, 'Towards a National Information Policy', *Bulletin of American Society of Information Science*, **2**(6):13–15, (1976).
2. Joan Spero, 'Information and Telecommunications is a Trade Issue', *Intermedia*, **10**(2):9–11 (1982); Alain Madec, 'The Political Economy of Information Flows', *ibid.*, **9**(2):29–32 (1981); and Francois Regis Hutin, 'Informatics is a Political Issue', *ibid.*, **9**(1):17–19, 1981.
3. Sajjad ur Rahman, 'Databases and Networks: Present Status and Prospects in the Muslim World', paper presented at the 2nd COMLIS conference, Malaysia, 20–22 October, 1986, p. 4–5.
4. M. Salleh Ashoor, 'Bibliographic Networking in the Arabian Gulf Region: Prospects and Problems for Information Exchange', paper presented at the 2nd COMLIS conference, Malaysia, 20–22 October, 1986.
5. Faria Zahawi, 'Access to Information in the Arab World: The Development of the Arab League Documentation Centre (ALDOC) and Plans of the Arab Information System Network (ARISNET)', paper presented at the 2nd COMLIS conference, Malaysia, 20–22 October, 1986.
6. See *Report of IFSTAD*, submitted to the Fifth Islamic Summit Conference, Kuwait, 26–28 January, 1987.
7. We have suggested a similar network for the Third World. See Ziauddin Sardar, 'Between GIN and TWIN: Meeting the Information Needs of the Third World', *Aslib Proceedings*, **33**(2):53–61 (1981).

10

Gate-Keepers and Purveyors of Ideas

Reponsibilities of Muslim Librarians and Information Scientists

Given the precarious times that we have inherited; the vast array of problems, from the provision of basic needs to eradication of illiteracy; the conspicuous absence of an indigenous knowledge based in Muslim countries; the social and intellectual inertia of Muslim societies themselves; as well as the disruptive impact that rapid developments in western technology are likely to have; given all these, and many other, components of the Muslim *problematique*: what is the function and responsibility of the information scientist towards his community?

Needless to say, Muslim librarians and information scientists would have to play a leading role in establishing an information infrastructure — and all information agencies, both distributive and centralized, which form the basis of such an undertaking — in the Muslim world. But apart from that, Muslim information scientists and librarians are uniquely qualified to fulfil a number of other important, not to say urgent, needs of the *ummah*. There are two specific roles that Muslim information scientists must adopt as their own territory: the first of which I would describe as civilizational gatekeepers; and the second as purveyors of ideas. To fulfil either of these functions adequately, Muslim information scientists have to see themselves as an integral part of a living civilization based on a dynamic world-view which has its own specific way of being, doing and knowing. While the world-view is there in its totality, the civilization based on it is seriously damaged by the ravages of history and is malfunctioning. Indeed, the damage is so serious that major reconstruction work and serious repair is needed; and unless this is urgently carried out the civilization faces the real threat of losing its integrity and holistic identity. Given the power of the new information technologies, it can even become an appendage to another, more powerful, alien civilization. It is in this work of reconstruction of Muslim civilization that the two unique roles of Muslim information scientists can best be seen.

As civilizational gatekeepers, Muslim information scientists have to behave rather like Janus, the Roman god of doorways.[1] Like Janus, they have to have two faces: one looking critically towards the sources of information, which are mostly within the confines of western civilization, and the other towards the users who are exclusively part of Muslim civilization. In his right hand, Janus held a staff to bar unwanted intruders: Muslim information scientists have to act as critical filters, barring irrelevant information. In his left hand Janus held a key — perhaps to the source of knowledge. Muslim information scientists must have the skills and expertise necessary to identify the most important and relevant sources of knowledge and information to save the valuable time and resources of researchers and students, intellectuals and thinkers. Janus was said to busy himself at the beginning of all enterprises — and when does one need information more than at the beginning of a research project or an intellectual endeavour? Janus also had the title of *convivius* meaning, the sower. Dissemination of information and ideas is indeed a major and one of the most fruitful activities of the information scientist.

All these functions are performed within a civilizational context. The prime function of the Muslim information scientist is reconstruction of his/her civilization; and he/she performs these activities with the ultimate goal in mind. As such, it is their responsibility to thwart any development which delays this work of reconstruction or which introduces new destructive elements which may undermine the full flowering of Muslim civilization. Thus, as civilizational gatekeepers, Muslim information scientists must use their conscious and critical judgement to promote that type of information which is most relevant to the needs and requirements of Muslim societies.

The role of Muslim information scientists as civilizational gatekeepers is intrinsically linked to their role as purveyors of ideas. Here the various units that go to form the civilization must be kept in full view: the basic units of any civilization are the individuals and their communities. The work of repairing and reconstructing Muslim civilization must start with fulfilling the needs of individuals and communities: healthy individuals and communities, ones with physical and mental health, will eventually produce a vigorous and intellectually thriving Muslim civilization. The means of communication that promotes this is not mass communication; it is not even microcomputers: it is the book, the learned journal and the serious magazine. It is the printed word, the word contained in books and journals, which enables a mind to communicate in depth with other minds and to ignore the limitations of time and space.

Indeed, Islamic culture, as our historical excursion in Chapter 2 demonstrates, is essentially the culture of the book. At the centre of the world-view of Islam, its very heart, is the Qur'an: the Noble Reading. It was because the Book of Guidance was the prime focus of Muslim civilization that the book and the whole range of activities related to it — writing, reading, calligraphy, copying, illustrating, binding, publishing, selling, storing, printing, cataloguing, preparing bibliographies, building libraries — became so central during the classical period of Islam. The book and its production was the key institution of the so-called Golden Age of Islam and one of its most refined arts.

In many respects, contemporary Muslim information scientists are counterparts of the classical *warraq* who formed a key link between the scholar and the public. The *warraqs* were an institution. Their basic job was to copy manuscripts and make them available to the scholarly community, a function that is nowadays performed collectively by the printer, publisher and the bookseller. But as an institution the *warraqs* did much more. They had complete command of the intellectual tools of their time; and, often, while copying manuscripts — which they did at a superhuman pace — they would add their own critical comments. Many of them were scholars in their own right: and copying manuscripts was a technique of mastering the contents. And because they had access to manuscripts across a range of disciplines, they acquired a wide base of knowledge. As such, the *warraqs* were true polymaths: they complemented a professional skill, which gave them prestige and economic support, with deep as well as wide knowledge. If a scholar desired to explore a certain disciplinary territory, the first professional he would consult would be the *warraq* who would not only point him in the right direction, but also offer criticism of other scholars as well as sell the appropriate manuscripts. The *warraqs* were the true purveyors of ideas.[2]

As modern counterparts of *warraqs*, the Muslim information scientists have to take over the niche left vacant in our society. They must have complete mastery of contemporary intellectual methods and have the ability to use it and assess the value of new contributions to knowledge to their society. Going much further than knowing the developments in their own area of speciality — librarianship, information science and their particular field of study — they should read adventurously, developing a keen awareness of those fields of knowledge which answer particular needs of their society and civilization. They should aim to serve not only research and scholarly communities, but also the individual thinker. They should serve as the catalysts for the intellectual development of the individual. Our culture, as the history of Islam demonstrates, does not develop in revolutions, nor through politics; but through the individual minds which form the basic components of society and through understanding and following particular ideas. Civilizations are not built only by heroes and great scholars, but also by ordinary people who have the humility and motivation to follow and learn through books and develop their minds. It is the wisdom of this central individual to understand, to direct, to cope with instability and insecurity, which ultimately determines the evolution of a society and a civilization. By developing their individuality and minds, that person also develops tolerance, humility, a concern for others, freedom from self-interest, self-discipline and goal-orientated behaviour. He/she becomes the foundation on which a civilization can be reconstructed.

What does the role of Muslim information scientists as civilizational gatekeepers and purveyors of ideas entail in specific terms?

Intellectual and Social Responsibilities

To perform the role of civilizational gatekeepers, even at the basic level, the first step that Muslim librarians and information scientists must take concerns their own field. The state of contemporary Muslim librarianship is abysmal: there are no classification schemes suitable for Islamic material, there are no rules for indexing Islamic literature, no thesauri, even the cataloguing of Muslim names appears to be an intellectually insurmountable problem. With the exception of the first, all of these problems can be solved simply by developing internationally accepted standards. The problems of producing appropriate classification schemes is a little more demanding.

It is worth noting at this stage, that the first Muslim philosopher, al-Kindi, was a librarian.[3] And like many librarians and philosophers of his period, classification was his major preoccupation. For them, the epistemology was the theoretical half of librarianship. And, as such, they devoted considerable energies to epistemology and sociology of knowledge. For al-Kindi, who produced the first Muslim classification of knowledge, the organization of information, the arrangement of books on a shelf, reflected the ideology of the organizer. And that is exactly how it is today.

Organization of information and knowledge is an ideological activity. Although this is not normally recognized, it is precisely why the major classification schemes of today — Dewey Decimal, Universal Decimal, Library of Congress — do not fit world-views other than that of western civilization. Witness the problems associated with classifying material on Islam or Buddhism or in one of the many oriental languages using these classification schemes.[4] The remarkable National Library of Turkey (*Milli Kutuphane*) in Ankara is an example *par excellence* of the difficulties associated with classifying material of an Islamic world view using the dominant occidental classification schemes.[5] Unable to use any scheme for their purpose, the librarian arranged books first by size, and then in the order in which they were received, in stacks closed to the public. They were catalogued by author and title, and there is a classified catalogue but subject sub-divisions are not at all detailed. The Russians, faced with similar difficulties and recognizing the ideological character of classification schemes some decades ago developed their own scheme based on the Marxist–Leninist world-view: BBK.

There is a direct relationship between the organization of information and knowledge, the human mind, and social behaviour. Information and knowledge organized on the basis of a particular world-view, will direct the mind towards that world-view and hence will influence the behaviour of those who have that organization imposed on them. To see one's entire culture, civilization and history relegated to a sub-sub-schedule, must give one a distorted view of oneself. Is not the domination of certain western classification schemes a sophisticated form of imperialism? For western classifications 'religion' or rather 'Islam' is one heading among others because in the western world-view, religion is one factor in a total pattern. But for Muslims, 'religion' is not one fact in a pattern but the pattern itself in all facets of human life. If you take religion away from a western person, the element of his/her life does not change; they simply cease to cohere into a meaningful whole. But Islam is not a factor in the life of a Muslim, it is the meaning that various factors of life have for him/her. Thus, western classification schemes, quite unwittingly, attack the essence of a Muslim being; they relegate the entire meaning of his/her existence into an insignificant sub-sub-heading. What greater injustice, or indeed, insult, could a Muslim suffer?

Muslim librarians and information scientists thus cannot rely on western classification schemes.[6] They must develop their own specialized classification schemes to give emphasis and meaning to their culture and history. There is no reason why the world should be dominated by a handful of classification schemes devised by the intellectual elites of the United States and Europe. While we need a general scheme for the classification of Islamic material throughout the Muslim world, we also need more specialized schemes for material in indigenous languages. A general classification scheme for Islam and the Muslim world, and a number of local classification schemes would only enrich the poverty-stricken fields of librarianship and information science. More new schemes would open new channels for research and understanding.

An interesting point on classification can be made concerning traditional societies which rely on symbols for communication. In western society, symbols play a rather small part. But in certain traditional societies they have a far more significant function; the traditional man of certain categories does not only think in symbols but actually participates in the reality they symbolize. This type of thinking is 'pre-logical': that is not to say that traditional men who use symbols cannot think logically, but that their way of knowing is not quite compatible with the western view of knowledge. However, reasoning and symbolism are not incompatible; but symbolism is not pure thought, and as such it is difficult to codify intellectual laws for it. Yet, it is a powerful way to articulate intense feeling and shared experience of the present. Symbolism is also a method of classification: it is a means by which traditional man 'harmonizes' himself, arranges his experiences, integrates into his society and the world as a whole. It validates social institutions and norms of conduct in a society. It is used for transmitting valuable information, from one human to another, from one group to another, and from one generation to another.

Earlier we argued that libraries are social agencies and mediators of desirable change. If they are to have a social impact, they must have a point of contract with the traditional man and his mentality. Symbolic classification schemes could be one such point of contact. By 'symbolic classification scheme' I mean schemes that are based on analysis of traditional symbolic thought patterns and which use, where desirable, symbolic notations.

To develop appropriate classification schemes for Islamic literature and indigenous material is a priority of Muslim librarians and information scientists. Without these schemes they cannot be true to either — their world-view or the material they handle.

In addition to developing unique classification schemes and indexing systems that are geared to meeting the demands of their material, Muslim information scientists and librarians, particularly in the perspective of our model of information and development, must also see themselves as educators. Purveyors of ideas are essentially educators.

The reading populace in the Muslim world consists mainly of clerical workers and students and includes candidates for public examinations. Thus functional reading dominates. Fiction is mostly translation and abridgements of popular European and American novels and romance. There is very little suitable fiction of local origin, although certain countries, notably Turkey, Pakistan, Egypt, Indonesia and Malaysia produce a reasonable output of fiction and other recreational reading matter. But much of this output is of little educational value.[7] The scarcity of reading material is not the sole reason for such a lack of interest in recreational reading. Some Muslim countries have established traditions of oral story-telling. However, there is no tradition of cultivating a reading habit. It is here that both public and school libraries have an important contribution to make.[8]

The common library users in Muslim countries are university graduates for whom reading is an exercise in the system of learning and information collecting. The reading habit has therefore to be cultivated, in both adults and children. School children exposed to reading while still at school will become the library users of the future. School librarians therefore have an important responsibility for the future of librarianship in the developing countries.

The school library is an integral part of a school: it must be a compulsory, dynamic part of the curriculum being worked out in the classroom. There are four basic functions of a library in a school:

1. To achieve greater growth and development of every child;
2. To cultivate a reading habit in every pupil;
3. To acquaint children with resource material — books, magazines, wall charts, films etc. — and its effective use;
4. To encourage in every child the habit of searching, finding out for himself or herself and critically evaluating information.

In all this the role of the librarian is as crucial as that of the teacher. The main object is to motivate the children to make full use of the library and its resources: both the teacher and the librarian are involved in this motivation. Only a coordinated effort by both of them can bring the full benefits of the school library to the pupils.

The fact that many librarians and information scientists see themselves as technicians rather than educators is a serious problem. This is due partly to the nature of their training; partly it is due to the lack of adequate definition of their function within an academic environment. Since the future will call for an increased diversity of roles — both in the Third World and the West, perhaps it will help if librarians and information scientists saw themselves flexible enough to take on any shape required by an academic environment.

There are many similarities between instructional technology and information science. Information science has already benefited from various theories of education, and comparative librarianship draws its methodology largely from comparative education. But we can make more direct comparisons also: both instructional technology and information science supply required amounts of information at a specific point. Both use similar techniques of information dissemination, have related problems in classification, acquisition, collection development and cataloguing.[9] It is not unreasonable, therefore, to argue that librarians and information scientists should take themselves more seriously as educators. The reverse is, of course, also true: information science is, as we have been at pains to point out, eclectic and syncretic and a natural place for an academic generalist to take a stand and make the most of the new interdisciplinary spirit.

Within the academic community librarians and information scientists must take a wider and more dynamic role. Complaining about lack of funds for libraries is only one of their roles; they must also actively influence the planning process, changes in the education curricula, and the direction of education policies. After all, the libraries and information centres are dependent on the policies of the institution that provide them with accommodation!

In developing countries the role of information scientists and librarians extends to the media, in particular to radio and television. They must be as concerned with what these facilities provide as they are with the services of libraries and information centres. With their awareness of the educational and information needs of the community they must critically review radio and television programmes and where necessary participate in the development of appropriate media policies.

The minority that can read does not fare well. The publishing industry in most Muslim countries is non-existent: fiction as well as most of the non-fiction, including all text books at undergraduate and high school levels, and reference books, are imported and it is worth noting that most of the imports are of rather poor quality. This is not only expensive in terms of foreign exchange, but it has devastating effect on local intellectual morale. Further, aggressive book import policies impose an alien culture and distort the character and form of the local population.

The publication industry in most developing countries is remarkably poor. Text books, reference books, fiction and popular non-fiction are infrequently published and are very poorly printed. No doubt some of these books discourage readers and force them to turn to imported material. The situation regarding magazines and journals is not much better either. Almost all are of the non-technical, popular and fiction type, and very expensive. Standards of journalism are shabby and the printing usually leaves the eyes only to weep with. In certain local languages which use Arabic script, the calligraphy which appears to have been done by several different people using several types of pen impedes the reader. Naturally, imported magazines and journals are given outright preference.

Yet many Muslim countries possess adequate resources to produce first-rate books and others could, with a little assistance from their more technically advanced neighbours, produce both fiction and non-fiction of high quality. What seems to be lacking is an awareness of the serious consequences of import policies, and an absence of determination and planned effort to develop indigenous authorship and the publishing industry. Within the Muslim world, Malaysia, Turkey and Egypt have reasonably developed publishing industries. However, the coverage, depth of treatment and quality of writing and printing is quite another matter. Here the new desk-top publishing technology could improve matters considerably.

In this context it is important that librarians and information scientists in Muslim countries focus their attention on developing indigenous publishing industries. The emphasis must be on promoting the writing of original books, in particular text books at all levels, translation of technical books into local languages and also on arrangements for local editions of foreign advanced texts and reference books at reasonable prices. In the implementation of this policy emphasis should be given to the promotion of local authorship, and to the enticement of able teachers and researchers to take a lead in the preparation of quality texts. Perhaps it may be necessary to set a trend, a fashion, so to speak, as well as monitor quality control and standards. In certain disciplines — agriculture, medicine, and biological sciences — foreign books do not deal adequately with local problems, and sometimes no mention is made of problems that are of particular local concern. Quite often they describe experiences that are outside the arena of the local population, life forms that cannot be examined in the country, social forces that do not operate in the society while parallel experiences are at hand. Thus the irrelevant is magnified out of all proportion, while the directly relevant is overlooked. Locally published books written and researched by indigenous authors, would promote a sense of confidence and closeness to their culture, environment and the subjects of study.

For the promotion of an indigenous publication industry it is also necessary that the writing of books, monographs and reviews, editing, printing and publishing are all accorded an adequate professional status. Editing, printing and publishing are highly skilled activities — a fact which is not often recognized in the Muslim world. The nature and scope of work involved in preparing a good textbook, is no less commendable than a serious research endeavour and deserves to be recognized as such. It would be a constructive step if learned bodies, research councils and professional societies in developing countries gave due recognition by awarding a small number of annual national awards to outstanding authors. Other incentives to promote writing could also be developed.

We now see that to function as civilizational gatekeepers and purveyors of ideas, Muslim librarians and information scientists have to work on many levels and perform many-sided and complex tasks. All this is in addition to the functions they are normally required to perform. However, given the situation in most Muslim countries, and if Muslim librarians and information scientists care about their societies and profession, they will, willingly or unwillingly, find themselves propelled into political, social and economic fields. There is no escaping this fact.

Muslim librarians and information scientists have to act on a twelve-point plan. They have to focus their energies towards:

1. Developing an open outlook and being aware of the fact that they have to take appropriate information to their users rather than wait for their users to come to them. Librarianship and information science are participatory and active professions, not isolated and passive disciplines.
2. Organizing their profession so that it reflects the world-view of Islam and the needs of their societies more appropriately — that means developing classification schemes for Islamic material and indigenous literature, and producing more appropriate rules for indexing and cataloguing.
3. Monitoring the flow of ideas stemming from the West and bringing the more appropriate and relevant ideas to the attention of intellectuals and thinkers. This can be done individually by word of mouth

as well as by publishing critical bibliographies, reviews on current trends in the arts, review essays and short notices as well as abstracts and bulletins on current concerns.

4. Bringing like-minded Muslim scholars and thinkers together. This can be achieved at a simple level by letter-writing, or, at a more sophisticated level, by organizing meetings and conferences.

5. Promoting the indigenous publication industry. Muslim information scientists should be involved at all levels with the local publication industry. They should develop a habit of encouraging, and where possible helping, scholars and thinkers to write and individuals to buy and read books. A Muslim information scientist who is not on the editorial board of at least one journal or magazine, or writing regularly for one, is not sufficiently professional.

6. Campaigning for establishing libraries, including mobile libraries, and information centres in villages and inner city areas. Here one should not always wait for government support; local resoures can be manipulated to establish small, viable libraries manned by local residents or villagers themselves.

7. Campaigning for the eradication of illiteracy. Indeed, Muslim information scientists should design and lead such campaigns.

8. Working for the dissemination of basic 'survival' information amongst the population: information concerning health and preventive care, environmental protection and occupational hazards, citizens' rights and social responsibilities. Here too much reliance should not be placed on the mass media: they are limited by time and space and their main value is in stimulation; also, they can easily be manipulated.

9. Campaigning for quality and educational material in the mass media. Nothing has had a more devastating impact on our culture, and thwarted the development of our creative individuals, than the mass transfer of American and European programmes to our television stations, and features and articles to our newspapers and magazines. Muslim information scientists should fight, both by word and deed, for increasing the proportion of local material in all components of the media.

10. Promoting the transfer of information between Muslim countries. Muslim information scientists should work towards setting up regional information networks — these need not be formal institutions, they could also be informal 'invisible colleges'. Moreover, they should extend across the whole range of appropriate disciplines.

11. Gaining the confidence of and involving themselves with policy formulators and decision-makers. They should actively seek advisory and consulting roles and must thoroughly immerse themselves in the environment — physical, social, cultural and intellectual — they are serving.

12. Developing a 'critical consciousness' in themselves and their clients in areas of mutual concern. This involves excursions into the scholarship of science and technology and more intensive and extensive involvement in review, criticism and evaluation of literature than has been practised so far.

Participation. Awareness. Dynamic involvement. Environmental immersion. Critical Consciousness. Campaigning outlook. Scholarship of science and technology. These are the determinants for librarians and information scientists practising their craft in a Muslim country. Of course, I am not suggesting that every Muslim information scientist should undertake to fulfil all the above responsibilities. Here the distinction made by Imam al-Ghazzali in *The Book of Knowledge* about *Fard-ul ayn* (individually requisite knowledge) and *Fard-ul Kifayah* (socially requisite knowledge) is particularly useful.[10] A complete knowledge of his/her own discipline, a mastery of contemporary intellectual tools, and a theoretical and practical understanding of the communication process is essential for Muslim information scientists: this can be considered to be *Fard-ul ayn*, without this basic equipment, an information scientist cannot be considered a true professional. The eight responsibilities delineated above come under *Fard-ul Kifaya*: it is not essential for every Muslim information scientist to work in all of these areas, but these responsibilities must be fulfilled collectively for they are essential for the survival of the whole Muslim *ummah*, for the reconstruction and re-emergence of Muslim civilization in our time.

Now, the question arises: what does this mean in terms of training and professional education?

Towards Appropriate Training

Once we understand the role of librarians and information scientists in its true perspective, it becomes relatively easy to discuss the education and professional training they need to fulfil their responsibilities. The conventional concentration of library and information science courses in cataloguing, indexing, classification, reprography, manipulation of computer files, library and information unit management constitutes the basic training. It is only the first step of the ladder: librarianship and information science must not stop there. That librarianship and information science courses have generally been isolated from social relevance and from conceptual criticism is a regrettable realization. This is even truer in Muslim countries where the library and information science schools are largely a colonial legacy and have uncritically and unwittingly adopted the curriculum and syllabi of the occidental universities; a point ably illustrated, among others, by Anis Khurshid.[11]

From the perspective of our model of information and development, it becomes essential for the concerns of ordinary life to be brought into the library and information syllabus, even at the expense of a certain tidiness in its organization. The future librarians and information scientists must feel that they are an active catalyst in the development process; that their job does not finish by delivering documents to the user; that their books, reports, journals, ideas, cataloguing, classification, thesauri, retrieval systems, computers and software are not ends in themselves but are tools to be used; that they have a responsibility towards the preservation of a nation's culture; that they have a responsibility to provide relevant material in a useful form; and that in the final analysis, they are also responsible for the side effects of the information they shuffle.

All this means that librarians and information scientists must have some familiarity with the language, tradition, culture, history and the problems of the people they are serving. Furthermore, they must be familiar with the world-view and outlook of their clients. Finally, they must have some understanding of how the development process operates. We must admit that these are difficult requirements: but then development is a complex process and in no aspect more so than in the furnishing of enlightened information to the people, policy formulators and decision-makers of Muslim countries.

It is obvious that the above educational criteria can best be fulfilled by indigenous library and information schools. Most developing countries have some kind of library and information training schools, where one does not exist it is necessary to establish one as soon as circumstances permit. The practice of sending students abroad for study should not be encouraged, for overseas courses are designed for different environments with different operative determinants. Students subjected to curricula of overseas schools acquire undue self-importance and status while their training has little relevance to the environment in which they will be working.[12]

Local library and information schools should operate on four principles. These principles will be hard for occidental institutions to accept as it is their domination, prestige and income that is threatened.[13]

1. Socially-aware courses that emphasize local needs, priorities and aspirations to a standard of education and qualification which makes information science a worthy and dynamic profession totally involved in the development process should be instituted.
2. All efforts should be made to develop local schools and training institutions if it becomes necessary to send students abroad when they should be sent to a neighbouring developing country which has similar problems, and to some degree, similar cultural and traditional background.
3. It must be specified in some form that the problems of Muslim countries and civilization are as important, challenging and intellectually taxing and as exciting as the problems of the western countries.
4. The students should be encouraged to find solutions to technical and economic problems of local information science in the context of optimum use of material and human resources in the country, and not by implementation of processes geared to the resource patterns of other societies.

These principles are designed to awaken consciousness and evolve a critical awareness of the student's professional identity, situation and role in society. The librarians and information scientists have to be trained to analyse causes and consequences, to act logically and reflectively, to perceive the reality of development, and to move to transform it. As such, they have to be very special persons; and their education and training must reflect these special qualities.

In the information age, the numerous challenges before the Muslim *ummah* are indeed formidable. Muslim librarians and information scientists have the responsibility, as well as the opportunity, to lead the way towards a viable recovery of Muslim identity and civilization. The realization of this challenge and opportunity begins with appropriate training and outlook.

Notes

1. The example of Janus is taken from J.S. Rippon, *Infomaniac*, City University, Department of Information Science, Spring 1975, p. 32.
2. For detailed study of the role performed by the *warraqs* see Johannes

Pederson, *The Arabic Book*, Geoffrey French (trans.), Princeton University Press, New Jersey, 1984.

3. George N. Atiyeh, *Al-Kindi: The Philosopher of the Arabs*, Rawalpindi, Islamic Research Institute, 1966.

4. See Ziauddin Sardar, *Islam: Outline of a Classification Scheme*, London, Clive Bingley, 1979.

5. Emily Dean, *Libraries in Turkey*, Ankara, n.d., (mimeographed).

6. For some of the problems that can arise in classification and cataloguing of Islamic material, see Peter Colvin, 'Organizing a Library in Libya', *Focus on International and Comparative Librarianship*, **9**(2):17–19, 1978.

7. See L. Matrai, 'Tradition and Innovation: Reading in a Changing Society', in *Reading in a Changing World*, F.E. Mohrhordt (ed.), Verlag Dokumentation, Munich, 1976.

8. For an interesting case study see F.A. Ogunsheye, 'Reading for Development in Urban Africa: The Case of Ibadan', in F.E. Mohrhordt, *op. cit.*

9. Basil Bernstein, 'On the Classification and Framing of Educational Knowledge', in *Knowledge and Control*, M. Young (ed.), Collier Macmillan, London, 1971.

10. Al-Ghazzali, *The Book of Knowledge*, Nabih Amin Fris (trans.), Lahore, Ashraf, 1962.

11. Anis Khurshid, 'Library Education in South Asia', *Libri*, **20**:59–79 (1970); and 'Standards for Library Science Education in Burma, Ceylon, India and Pakistan', *Herald of Library Science Documentation*, **17**:23–34, (1970).

12. Cf. R.C. Benge, *Libraries and Cultural Change*, Clive Bingley, London, 1970, p. 200:

> Needless to say there are on the other hand formidable arguments in favour of continuing the overseas nexus as long as possible. Firstly, there is always local opposition to an indigenous qualification because there is the feeling that the qualification may find internal recognition slow, and external recognition non-existent or reluctant. Secondly it is natural that students themselves usually prefer to study abroad — and a library school at home may seem to rule this out. The answer is to ensure that the necessary overseas experiences should be gained *after* the basic qualification — although it may be difficult or even undesirable to arrange a trip abroad for everyone. Thirdly, it may well happen that it is difficult to *guarantee* continuous development for a national library school. Breakdowns may occur because of difficulties in obtaining lecturers, or the libraries may reach saturation point with regard to qualified staff. In smaller countries the demand for library personnel is so limited that a national school cannot be supported.

13. Cf: H.M. Kibirige, 'Current Trends in the Training of Library and Information Specialists in East Africa', *Libri* **25**(1):34–39 (1975). The Enugu Seminar, Mr. Kibirige reports, identified four basic aims of an African school of librarianship:

   (a) To provide a standard of education and qualification which would make librarianship a profession worthy of ranking alongside other traditional professions.

   (b) To pay special attention to the library needs of the future.

(c) To adapt existing teaching practices where necessary to suit local circumstances.
(d) To be responsible for publication of original material specially concerned with African problems.'

See also, 'Regional Conference on the Development of Public Libraries in Africa', *UNESCO Bulletin for Libraries* **27**(2) March–April, 1963.

Conclusion

Building Blocks of an Islamic Information Policy

The new technologies of information and communication confront the Muslim world with a frightening dilemma. On the one hand, if the new technologies are totally ignored, as they are at the moment, they could lead to a hitherto unimagined form of dependency and colonialism. On the other hand, the development in these areas is so rapid and the technology so complex that it is not possible for any Muslim country to acquire and develop these technologies independently of the industrialized countries. Moreover, these technologies are a double-edged sword: even if they could be acquired at an acceptable economic cost, their social, cultural, intellectual and political ramifications could be devastating. Thus the Muslim world faces the daunting challenge of acquiring appropriate information and communication technologies and using them to promote healthy development of Muslim societies, culture and people.

Meeting this challenge requires developing information structures that synthesize the traditional with the modern within individual Muslim countries as well as within the Muslim world itself. The evolution of this infrastructure must be based on an integrated strategy that derives its legitimacy from the world-view of Islam. As such, the use of new information and communication technologies, as well as the upgrading of traditional systems, must be made subject to such conceptual indicators of the world-view of Islam as *tawheed, adl, shura, ijma, istislah, hikma* and *ummah*. Only by guiding ourselves with these values can we make appropriate decisions about the utility and usefulness of information for Muslim societies. Such a strategy also requires a new paradigm of development: a basic needs orientated approach based on the notions of self-reliance and community participation, social justice and cultural authenticity. Information plays a vital role in this notion of development; and the provision of adequate, appropriate and timely information to all segments of society is an essential prerequisite for survival in the next century.

A sensible information strategy for the Muslim world designed to meet the demands of the twenty-first century would thus have the following seven features:

1. Since much information that is generated in the modern world has little relevance to Muslim societies, Muslim countries would have to focus on generating their own information and knowledge base. This becomes even more urgent given that information is rapidly becoming a major source of power, and access to information would shape the destiny of states in the future. As such, it is necessary for Muslim countries to generate their own information; that is, Muslim countries must develop self-sufficiency in local, relevant and significant R and D capabilities as well as domestic technological self-reliance. The experience of three decades of conventional strategies of development has shown that reliance on external sources leads to a particularly ugly form of dependency and ushers in a new form of colonialism. It is thus necessary for Muslim countries to establish indigenous research and development institutions and promote original and relevant pure and applied research in all areas of human endeavour. To overcome the need for scarcity of resources and trained manpower, Muslim countries should cooperate in joint scientific and technological strategy and pool their resources. This is dictated by the Islamic notions of *hikma* (wisdom) and *shura* (consultation, cooperating for the good).

2. There is a need for every Muslim country to develop an appropriate information structure. The role of the centralized component of this infrastructure is to synthesize and make available relevant information to national users. The centralized components of this structure should consist of: a national library and documentation centre; specialized information centres on science and technology, medicine, agriculture, business and finance, legal information, and other areas of specific concern to individual countries; a centre for information

transfer to act as an information exchange linking users with sources of information; and a national standards institution. This is derived from the Islamic notion of *istislah* (public interest) and *ijma* (consensus; synthesis).

3. The decentralized components of the infrastructure must focus on: (a) services by which citizens can develop their ability to participate in national decision-making processes; (b) mechanisms by which individuals and communities should be able to consult and cooperate on matters of common concern; (c) services that provide free and easy access to information for citizens on matters that affect them such as legal rights, environmental issues, national and public policy concerns and on matters which would help communities face every day problems. This involves setting up a network of public, rural and mobile libraries as well as consumer information centres and information centres designed to provide access to more general information ·which could help citizens deal wih daily concerns. This is dictated by the Islamic notions of *adl* (social justice) and *istislah* (public interest).

4. The needs of Muslim scientists, technologists and scholars require special attention as they carry the responsibility for laying the foundations for a Muslim civilization of the future. Here the emphasis must shift from the transfer of information from the industrialized countries to communication of science within the *ummah*; this is the only viable cure for the isolation and suffocation of Muslim scientists and thinkers. Only genuine communication with their peers can make the work of Muslim scientists and thinkers more relevant to the needs and requirements of Muslim societies and culture. Unless there is an adequate system for the communication of science within the Muslim world, along with an appropriate information structure, we cannot expect our scientists, technologists and scholars to fulfil the responsibility that we place on their shoulders. The need to meet the information needs of the scholars is a requisite of the notion of *ilm* (distributive knowledge) and the respect that the world-view of Islam gives to its *ulama* (seekers after knowledge).

5. To meet the growing information needs of Muslim states and individual researchers and scholars, it is necessary to establish an international Muslim information network and a specialized international referral service. The former would provide a medium for access to and exchange of information, generated within the Muslim countries as

well as relevant information produced in industrialized countries, relating to science, technology, medicine, agriculture, industry, business and finance. It would link various national libraries and specialized information centres and would involve cooperation between Muslim countries. The latter would focus on the specific needs of Muslim scholars and would function on the level of international organizations. It would bring together the rapidly increasing literature on the 'Islamization of knowledge' and the traditional areas of Islamic studies; it would link Muslim scholars working in isolated enclaves, to build the intellectual foundation of a Muslim civilization of the future. The establishment of such international networks is based on the Islamic notions of the *ummah* (international Muslim community, the civilization of Islam), which should behave as an integrated and holistic organism, and *shura* (consultation, cooperating for the good).

6. Muslim librarians and information scientists have a special role to play in meeting the challenges of the information age. They must see themselves as an integral part of a living civilization based on a dynamic world-view, with its own specific way of being, doing and knowing, but which has been damaged and is in need of reconstruction. They must fulfil the role of civilizational gatekeepers, controlling the flood of irrelevant information coming from the industrialized countries, and as purveyors of ideas they must become the counterpart of the classical polymath, synthesizing ideas and examining the developments of knowledge from a broad, general perspective. One of the major challenges they face involves bringing the book back to the central position it once held in Muslim civilization. As such they must play an active part in promotion reading and the indigenous publishing industry. It is also the responsibility of Muslim librarians and information scientists to ensure that information and knowledge on traditions, traditional cultures and traditional world-views filters down to the level of individual citizens. Moreover, they have to convey and present modern knowledge and contemporary innovations to the citizens in a manner that does not undermine the existing cultural establishment. These roles for librarians and information scientists in Muslim societies is derived from the Islamic notions of *khilafah* and *amana* (trusteeship; the institutions in their care are a trust — *amana* — which they must look after and put at the service of the users in the most creative and beneficial way) and *ummah* of which they are the appropriate guardians.

7. In setting up national information structures, centralized and
distributive, as well as *ummah*-wide networks, providing information
to rural areas and promoting the local publications industry, the most
effective and economically viable information and communication
technologies should be used. Muslim countries should cooperate to
develop appropriate technologies, and where this is not possible, to
adopt and modify existing technologies to fit their specific needs and
requirements. Almost all developments in information technology
have been instrumental in the fragmentation of science and
quantization of human beings. It is therefore necessary that we take a
more synthetic and holistic approach to information, and become
aware of the philosophical, cultural and subjective dimension of
information. The Muslim decision-makers and planners, scholars
and intellectuals, librarians and information scientists, have a great
role to play in clothing information with knowledge and wisdom.
This is encouraged by the Islamic notion of *hikma* (wisdom), *shura*
(cooperation for the good) and *ijma* (consensus and synthesis).

Any information strategy for the Muslim world must take into
account the need to protect ourselves from too much external stimuli; too
much information is just as manipulative as dependency on external
information sources. At present, there seems to be at once too much
information and too little information: there is abundance, indeed super-
abundance, of worthless, obnoxious, even manipulative information,
and a scarcity of relevant, high-quality information. The abundance of
manipulative information is the result of information transfer from the
industrialized countries which research has shown to be largely irrelevant to the needs and requirements of Muslim countries. The lack of
quality information is due to suffocation of indigenous scientific talent
and authorship and the absence of a local publication industry, as well as
any means for Muslim countries to share their resources on a *ummah*-
wide basis. There is a need, on the one hand, to fight the degradation of
our moral and social environment, and, on the other, to develop local
and international avenues and channels of indigenous self-expression.

The challenges that the information age has cast before the Muslim
world can be successfully met only by giving a practical shape to the
central concepts and values of Islam. Information technologies present
us with some very tricky and complex choices: only by taking charge of
the situation, and guiding ourselves by the conceptual operators and
value parameters of Islam can we avoid waking up one day, some time in
the distant future, to discover that we have lost the independence and

integrity that we fought for decades to achieve. It is indeed ironic that an historical epoch noted for its lack of concern for eternal values now confronts us with formidably interlinked problems which can be solved only by going forward to the pragmatic values of the world-view of Islam.

Bibliography

Abdul Haq, A.M. 'International Librarianship and Library Development in Bangladesh', *Focus on International and Comparative Librarianship*, **8** (2) 15–17 (1977).

——and Aman, Mohammed M. *Librarianship and the Third World: An Annotated Bibliography of Selected Literature on Developing Nations, 1960-1975*, New York, Garland, 1977.

Abras, M. 'Financial Allocation of the Libraries of Teachers' Training Institutes in Jordan', *Risalat-al-Maktaba*, **12** (July 1977).

Adedigba, Yakub A. 'Forestry Researchers as Information Users in Nigeria', *Information Development* **1** 229–33 (October 1985).

Agha, Stella J. 'Constraints on Library Automation in Nigeria', *Information Development*, **2** 159–62 (July 1986).

Ahmad, Khurshid. 'Economic Development in An Islamic Framework' in Islamic Perspectives: *Studies in Honour of Sayyid Abul Ala Mawdudi*, Khurshid Ahmad and Zafar Ishaq Ansari (eds.), Islamic Foundation, Leicester, 1979.

Ahmed, N. 'Education for Librarianship in Bangladesh', *International Library Review* **13** 103–15 (January 1981).

Ahmed, Sultanuddin. 'National Information Scene in Bangladesh', *Indian Library Association Bulletin* **15** 111–15 (July–Dec 1979).

Ahsan, Muhammad Manazir and Anees, Munawar Ahmad. 'Contemporary Islamic Resurgence — A Select Bibliography (1979–1982)', *Muslim World Book Review*, **2**(4) 55–67 (1982).

Aina, Lenrie O. 'Agricultural Information Provision in Nigeria', *Information Development*, **2** 242–44 (October 1986).

El-Akhras, Mahmud. 'ALECSO and Special Library Collections in the Arab Countries', *UJISLAA*, **3**(1) 55–9 (1981).

Alabi, G.A. 'Library Automation in Nigerian Universities', *Information Development*, **2** 163–5 (July 1986).

Ali, M.M. 'Muslims in Britain — A Comprehensive Bibliography', *Muslim World Book Review* **6**(2) 51–64 (1986).

Aman, Mohammad M. 'Bibliographical Services in Arab Countries', *College and Research Libraries*, **31** 249–59 (July 1970).

——. 'School Libraries in the Arab States', in *School Libraries International Development*, Jean Lowerie (ed.) Metuchen, New Jersey, Scarecrow Press, 1972.

——. 'Arab Countries' in *International Handbook of Contemporary Developments in Librarianship*, Miles M. Jackson (ed.), Westport, Greenwood Press, 1981.

——. 'Egypt, Libraries in', in *Encyclopedia of Library and Information Science*, Allen Kent, *et al.* (eds.), New York, Marcel Dekker, 1972, Vol. 7, pp. 574–88.

——. 'Library and Information Science Education in the Muslim World', in *Library Education Across the Boundaries of Cultures . . .*, Anis Khurshid (ed.) Karachi, Department of Library Science, University of Karachi, 1981.

——. 'Egyptian University Libraries', *Library History Review*, **2** 1–9 (March 1975).

——. *Documentation and Library Services of the Ministry of Information*, UNESCO Report prepared for the Government of the Hashemite Kingdom of Jordan, Paris, UNESCO, 1980.

——. *Arab Periodicals and Serials: A Bibliography*, New York, Garland, 1979.

——. (ed.) *Cataloging and Classification of Non-Western Materials: Concerns, Issues and Practices*, Phoenix, Oryx Press, 1980.

Aman, Mohammed M. and Zehery, M. *Kuwait University Libraries: A Study and Recommendation for Improvement — Final Report*, Kuwait, Kuwait University Press, 1978.

al-Amin, A. 'Training of Librarians in Iraq', *Risalat-al-Maktaba*, **12** (July 1977).

Anees, Munawar Ahmad. 'Arabic Word Processing — Writing the Right Way', *Inquiry*, **3**(9) 53–7 (1986).

——. 'Automated Information for Islamic Studies — A Future Imperative?', paper presented at the Congress of Muslim Librarians and Information Scientists, Universiti Utara Malaysia, 20–2 October 1986, Kedah, Malaysia.

——. 'Bibliographers — Endangered Species?' *Inquiry*, **3**(3) 68–9 (1986).

——. 'Computers for Quranic Studies', *Impact International*, **13**(11) 14 (1983).

——. 'Facilitating Access to Islamic Material', *Inquiry*, **4**(5) 24–31 (1987).

——. 'Information for Cultural Survival', *Inquiry*, **3**(1) 46–9 (1986).

——. 'Islamic Studies — Publish and Perish? Book and Periodical Citations on Tafsir al-Quran in Western Languages', *Muslim World Book Review*, **5**(2) 55–68 (1985).

——. 'Translating the Untranslatable?' *Inquiry*, **3**(5) 68–9 (1986).

——. 'Utilization of Computer Technology in Islamic Studies', Search: Journal for Arab and Islamic Studies, **4**(1–2) 73–6 (1983).

——and Athar, Alia Nasreen. *Guide to Sira and Hadith Literature in Western Languages*, London, Mansell, 1986.

—— ——. 'Significance of Scientific, Technical and Social Information for the Muslim World', *Journal Rabetat al-Alam al- Islami*, **7**(8) 25–9 (1980).

Anwar, Mumtaz A. *Urban Public Libraries in Pakistan*, Lahore, Publishers United Limited, 1983.

——. 'Towards a Universal Bibliographic System for Islamic Literature',

International Library Review, **15**(3) 257–61 (1983).

——. *Information Services in Muslim Countries*, London, Mansell, 1985.

——. 'Bibliographical Control of Academic Dissertations in Muslim Countries', Paper presented at the Congress of Muslim Librarians and Information Scientists, 20–22 October 1986, Kedah, Malaysia.

——. *National Libraries in the Muslim World: A Bibliography*, London, Mansell, 1987.

Asali, J.J. 'Jordan, Libraries in', in *Encyclopedia of Library and Information Science*, Allen Kent, *et al.*, (eds.) New York, Marcel Dekker, 1975, Vol. 13, pp. 300–10.

Ashoor, M. Salleh. 'Bibliographic Networking in the Arabian Gulf Region: Prospects and Problems for Information Exchange', Paper presented at the Congress of Muslim Librarians and Information Scientists, 20–22 October 1986, Kedah, Malaysia.

——. 'The Formation of Muslim Names', *International Library Review*, **9** 491–500 (1977).

Aslam, Muhammad. 'Special Libraries in Pakistan', *Special Libraries*, **68** 161–4 (April 1977).

Atiyeh, George N. *Al-Kindi: The Philosopher of the Arabs*, Rawalpindi, Islamic Research Institute, 1966.

Awad, Twefik. 'School Libraries in the Arab Republic of Egypt', *Unesco Bulletin for Libraries*, **26** 241–7 (July 1972).

——. 'Bibliographical Services in Egypt in 1971', *Bibliography, Documentation, Terminology*, **13** 13–14 (January 1973).

Badr, Ahmad. 'Kuwait, Libraries in', in *Encyclopedia of Library and Information Science*, Allen Kent, *et al.* (eds.) New York, Marcel Dekker, 1975, Vol. 14, pp. 1–18.

——. and Kalendar, Sulaiman. 'Kuwait University Libraries', *Unesco Bulletin for Libraries*, **24** 79–82 (March–April 1970).

Bakalla, M.H. *Arabic Linguistics: An Introduction and Bibliography*, London, Mansell, 1983.

Barnes, Robert F. 'Information and Decision', in *Perspectives in Information Science*, Anthony Debons and William J. Cameron (eds.), Leyden, Noordhoff, 1975.

Begdikian, B. *The Information Machine*, New York, 1971.

Bell, Daniel. *The Coming of the Post-Industrial Society*, Basic Books, New York, 1973.

Bell, S. 'Information Systems Planning and Operation in Less Developed countries. Part 2: Case Study, Information Systems, Evaluation', *Journal of Information Science*, **12** 319–32 (1986).

——. 'Information Systems Planning and Operation in Less Developed Countries. Supplement', *Journal of Information Science*, **12** 333–6 (1986).

Benge, Ronald C. *Cultural Crisis and Libraries in the Third World*, Clive Bingley, London, 1979.

——. *Libraries and Cultural Change*, Clive Bingley, London, 1970.

Bernstein, Basil. 'On the Classification and Framing of Educational Knowledge', in *Knowledge and Control*, M. Young (ed.), Collier Macmillan, London, 1971.

Bin Dobaish, Abdul Latif. 'Libraries of Madina al-Munawarah (During the Ottoman Period)', *Pakistan Library Bulletin*, **1** 112–19 (March–June 1980).

——. 'Public and Private Libraries in the Hijaz Upto 1925', *Pakistan Library Bulletin*, **10** 17–25 (January–April 1979).

Binark, Ismet and Eren, Halit. *World Bibliography of Translations of the Meanings of the Holy Qur'an — Printed Translations 1515–1980*, Istanbul, Research Centre for Islamic History, Art and Culture, 1986.

Birou, A. *et al.*, Towards a Re-Definition of Development, Pergamon Press, Oxford, 1977.

Biswas, Ahsan A. 'Bangladesh National Scientific and Technical Documentation Centre: Functions and Activities', *Journal of Library and Information Science (India)*, **2** 69–73 (June 1977).

Bosch, G., Carswell, John, and Petheridge, Guy. *Islamic Bookbindings and Bookmaking*, The Oriental Institute Museum, The University of Chicago, 1981.

Botros, Salib. 'Problems of Book Development in the Arab World with Special Reference to Egypt', *Library Trends*, **26** 567–74 (Spring 1978).

Brewster, Beverley J. 'A Student Reference Service: The Pahlavi Experiment', *International Library Review*, **10** 411–26 (October 1978).

Brioleon, L. *Science and Information Theory*, Paris, 1949.

Capurro, Rafael. 'Moral Issues in Information Science', *Journal of Information Science*, **11**(3) 113–24 (1985).

Cawkell, A.E. 'The Real Information Society: Present Situation and Some Forecasts', *Journal of Information Science*, **12**(3) 87–96 (1986).

CENTO, *Regional Documentation Centres Conference*, 29 April–1 May 1974, CENTO Scientific Programme Report No. 12, 1975.

Chandler, George. *Libraries in the East: An International and Comparative study*, London, New York, Seminar Press, 1971.

——. 'Near Middle East and the Far East Libraries, *International Library Review*, **3** 187–227 (April 1971).

Colvin, Peter. 'Organizing a Library in Libya', *Focus on International and Comparative Librarianship*, **9**(2) 17–19 (1978).

Consumer Association of Penang, *Third World: Development or Crisis*, Penang, 1984.

Deale, Vail. 'Librarianship in Iran', *College and Research Libraries*, **27** 461–3 (November 1966).

Dean, Emily. *Libraries in Turkey*, Ankara, n.d., (mimeographed).

Deblas, Ismail. 'School Libraries in Salt: Problems and Solutions', (In Arabic) *Risalat-al-Maktaba*, **15** (December 1980).

Druker, P. *Managing in Turbulent Times*, Harper and Row, New York, 1981.

Eliot, T.S. *The Four Quarters*, Faber and Faber, London, 1944.

Emdad, Ali Akbar. *Survey of Library Utilization by the Students of Pahlavi University*, MLS thesis, Shiraz, Pahlavi University, School of Graduate Studies, 1977.

Eres, B.K. 'Transfer of Information Technology to Less Developed Countries: A Systems Approach', *Journal of the American Society for Information Science*, **32**(3) 97–102 (1981).

Eyro, John J. *Republic of Afghanistan: Library Development (NATIS)*, Paris, UNESCO, 1977, p. 58 (Technical Report pp. 1975–76/4. 221–4).

Farsouni, Faud. 'Bibliographical Organisation in the Successive Jordanian Legislations', (In Arabic), *Risalat-al-Maktaba*, **15** (December 1980).

Farvn, M.P., and Milton, J.P. (eds.), *Careless Technology*, The National History Press, New York, 1972.

Fashah, Issa I. 'Arab Libraries in Jordan and Israel', *California Librarian*, **38** 48–54 (January 1977).

Fatin, Inayat. 'Computers and Libraries in Arab Countries', (In Arabic), *Risalat-al-Maktaba*, **13** 26–34 (19 June 1978).

Feather, Frank and Rushmi Mayur. 'Communications for Global Development: Closing the Information Gap' in *Communication and the Future: Prospects, Promise and Problems*, Howard F. Didsbury, World Future Society, Washington D.C. 1982.

Galtung, J. *et al.* (eds.), *Self-Reliance: A Strategy for Development*, Bogle-L'Overture, London, 1980.

Gandon, Francis. 'La Lecture Publique en Algeria: l'example d'Oran', *Mediatheques Publiques*, **46** 39–44 (April–June 1978).

———. National Library for Bangladesh, *International Library Review*, **9** 95–112 (January 1977).

Ghaheri, Hamid. *Survey of the Activities of the Department of Libraries and Their Relationship to the Collections and Services of High School Libraries in Kuwait*, MLS thesis, Shiraz, Pahlavi University, School of Graduate Studies, 1976.

Al-Ghazzali, *The Book of Knowledge*, translated by Nabih Amin Fris, Lahore, Ashraf, 1962.

El-Hadi, M.M. 'Library and Information Services in Egypt, 1979', in *Bowker Annual of Library and Book Trade Information, 1980*. 25th edn. New York, Bowker, 1980.

Haider, Syed Jalaluddin. 'University Libraries in Iran', *Libri*, **24** 102–3 (February 1974).

———. 'Medical Information in Pakistan', *International Library Review*, **13** 117–28 (January 1981).

———. 'Pakistan Librarianship in 1970s — Current Trends and Emerging Issues', *Libri*, **33**(3) 208–35 (1983).

———. 'Science and Technology Libraries in Pakistan', *Special Libraries*, **65** 474–78 (October–November 1974).

———. 'Status of Library Research in Pakistan', *Libri*, **28** 326–7 (December 1978).

———. 'University Libraries in Pakistan', *College and Research Libraries*, **36** 319–83 (Sept 1975).

———. 'Libraries in Ancient and Medieval Iran', *Pakistan Library Bulletin*, **8** 26–40 (July–October 1977).

———. 'Scientific Research and Information Facilities in Iran', *Special Libraries*, **67** 104–10 (February 1976).

Hamshari, Omar Ahmed Muhammed. 'Cataloguing in Publication and the National Jordanian Bibliography', (In Arabic), *Risalat-al-Maktaba*, **15** (December 1980).

———. *Libraries in Jordan: Proposed Applications of UBC and Related Concepts for Their Future Development*, MLS thesis, Loughborough, Loughborough University, 1980.

———. 'Library and Information Science', *Risalat-al-Maktaba*, **12** (June 1977).

Hanif, Akhtar. 'Development of Children's Libraries in Pakistan', *Pakistan Library Bulletin*, **10** 16–22 (December 1979).

Haroon, Muhammad. *Cataloguing of Indian Muslim Names*, Delhi, Indian Bibliographic Bureau, 1984.

Harvey, John F. 'International Library Report Implementation', *International Library Review*, **12** 115–25 (April 1980).

——. 'Iranian Health Science Libraries in Revolution', *International Library Review*, **13** 221–7 (April 1981).

——. 'Iranian Library Update', *Library Journal*, **104** 2288–9 (1 November 1979).

——. 'Proposal for a National Library Plan for Iran', *International Library Review*, **2** 253–61 (July 1970).

——. 'Tehran Mosques Libraries and a Comparison with American Christian Church Libraries', *International Library Review*, **13** 385–95 (October 1981).

——. 'Iran', in *International Handbook of Contemporary Developments in Librarianship*, Westport, Conn. Greenwood Press, 1981.

——. 'Iranian Health Science Libraries in Revolution', *International Library Review*, **13** 222 (April 1981).

Higgin, G. 'Information Management: Taking Account of the Human Element', *Aslib Proceedings*, **37**(2) 91–8 (1985).

Husain, Mahmud. *Of Libraries and Librarians in Pakistan*, University of Karachi, Karachi, 1974.

Hussain, Asaf. *Islamic Movements in Egypt, Pakistan and Iran: An Annotated Bibliography*, Mansell, London, 1983.

Hutin, F.R. 'Informatics is a Political Issue', *Intermedia*, **9**(1) 17–19, 1981.

Ibn Khaldun, *The Muqaddimah: An Introduction to History*, translated by F. Rozenthal, Routledge and Kegan Paul, London, 1967.

Iftekar Ali, Syed. 'Arab League Educational Cultural and Scientific Organization (ALECSO) and its Contribution to Middle Eastern Libraries', *International Library Review*, **17** 67–75 (1985).

Imamuddin, S.M. *Some Leading Muslim Libraries of the World*, Dhaka, Islamic Foundation Bangladesh, 1983.

Inayatullah, S. 'Bibliophilism in Medieval Islam', *Islamic Culture*, **12**(2) 154–69 (1938).

Independent Commission on International Development Issues, *North–South: A Programme for Survival*, Pan Books, London, 1980; and *Common Crisis, North–South: Cooperation for World Recovery*, Pan Books, London, 1983.

Jacos, Peter. 'Computerizing Information Services in Iraq', *Information Development* **2** 85–92 (April 1986).

Jafar, Mehrad. *A National Public Library System for Iran: A Descriptive Analysis 1948-1978 and a Plan for Development*, Ann Arbor, University Microfilms, 1979.

Jafar, Shahar Banun and Omar, Siti Mariani. 'Bibliographical Program and documentation of Islamic Materials in Malaysia', Paper presented at the Congress of Muslim Librarians and Information Scientists, 20–22 October 1986, Kedah, Malaysia.

Jirgis, George Amin. 'Special Libraries in Developing Countries', (Egypt), *Iranian Library Association Bulletin*, **10**(3) (Autumn 1977).

Joedono, S. 'Indonesia: Information Service Policy Objectives', *Baca*, **4**(3) 87–95 (1977).

Jogreshteh, Fazlolla. 'Public Libraries of Mazandaran Province', *Iranian Library Association Bulletin*, **10**(4) (Winter 1978).

Kamaruddin, Abdul Rahman. 'Perspectives for Development of an Islamic

Information System Network, Islamnet', Paper presented at the Congress of Muslim Librarians and Information Scientists, 20–22 October 1986, Kedah, Malaysia.

Karim, K.M. 'Library Network and Inter-Library Loan, Bangladesh', *International Library Review*, **12** 87–9 (July 1980).

Kaser D. *et al.*, *Library Development in Eight Asian Countries*, Metuchen, New Jersey, 1969.

Kashani, Zahra-Safe. *National Library of Iran*. MLS thesis, Shiraz, Pahlavi University, School of Graduate Studies, 1977.

Kautsky, J.A. *The Political Consequences of Modernization*, New York, Wiley, 1972.

Keshmiri, M.S. *et al.* 'Education for Librarianship at Pahlavi University, Shiraz, Iran', *International Library Review*, **11** 259–67 (April 1979).

Khalaf Nadim, *et al.* 'Economics of American University of Beirut Library', *Libri*, **28** 58–82 (March 1978).

Khalifa, Sha'ban. 'Libraries in Saudi Arabia', *Leads*, **20** 1–5 (March 1978).

——. *Libraries and Librarianship in Egypt*, Jeddah, Saudi Arabia, 1978.

Khalik, Azini. 'Current Legal Research in Malaysia', *International Journal of Law Librarians*, **7** 221–8 (November 1979).

Khan, Muhammad A.S. (comp.). *Directory of Islamic Libraries and Librarians*, Simi Valley, Cal. Islamic Library Association, 1983.

Khan, Muhammad Akram. *Islamic Economics — Annotated Sources in English and Urdu*, Leicester, The Islamic Foundation, 1982.

Khan, Sadiq Ali (ed.). *Proceedings of the Pakistan Library Association's 11th Conference, 16–18 October 1979*, Karachi, Khurshid Nishan, 1979.

Al-Kharafi, F., el-Rayyes, N. and Janini, G. 'Science Research in Kuwait — A Bibliometric Analysis', *Journal of Information Science*, **13** 37–44 (1987).

Khuda Bukhsh. *Islamic Studies*, Lahore, Sind Sagar Academy, undated reprint of 1926.

——. 'The Islamic Libraries', *The Nineteenth Century*, **52** 125–39 (1902).

Khurshid, Anis. 'Asian Librarianship', in *The Library in Society*, A. Robbert Regers *et al.*, (eds) Littleton, Libraries Unlimited, 1984.

——. 'Library Education in South Asia', *Libri*, **20** 59–79 (1970).

——. 'Access to Information for Research on Islam', Paper presented at the Congress of Muslim Librarians and Information Scientists, 20–22 October 1986, Kedah, Malaysia.

——. 'The Far East Libraries', In *Encyclopaedia of Library and Information Science*, Vol. 37, supplement 2, 1984, pp. 107–38.

——. (ed.). *Library Education Across the Boundaries of Cultures: a Festschrift*, Karachi, Library Science Department, University of Karachi, 1981.

——. 'Development of Cataloguing and Classification in Pakistan', in *Cataloguing and Classification of Non-Western Language Material*, M.M. Aman (ed.), Phoenix, Arizona, Oryx Press, 1980.

——. 'Problems of Bibliographical Accessibility of South Asian Collections', *International Library Review*, **15** 61–93 (January 1983).

——. 'Problems of Libraries in Pakistan', *Herald Library Science*, **20** 155–60 (July–Oct 1981).

——. 'Resource Sharing of University Libraries in Pakistan', *Herald Library Science*, **21** 169–79 (July–October 1982).

——. 'Standards for Library Education in Burma, Ceylon, India and Pakistan',

Pittsburgh, University of Pittsburgh, 1969, pp. 185–89; 237–83; 349–92; 414–21. Updated in *Encyclopaedia of Library and Information Science*, Vol. 21, 1977, pp. 255–99.

———. *The State of Library Resources in Pakistan*, Lahore, Student Services, 1982; 2nd ed., 1984.

Khurshid, Zahiruddin. *Libraries and Librarianship in Saudi Arabia*, Karachi, Mahmood Khan, 1980.

———. (comp.). *Ten Years Work in Librarianship in Pakistan: 1973–1983*, Karachi, Mahmood Khan, 1983.

———. *Libraries and Librarianship in Saudi Arabi*, Karachi, Mahmood Khan, 1980.

———. 'Libraries and Information Centres in Saudi Arabia', *International Library Review*, **11** 409–19 (October 1979).

Kibirige, H.M. 'Current Trends in the Training of Library and Information Specialists in East Africa', *Libri*, **25**(1) 34–9 (1975).

Al-Kindilchie, Amer I. 'Iraq, Libraries in', in *Encyclopedia of Library and Information Science*, Allen Kent, *et al.*, (eds.) New York, Marcel Dekker, 1975 Vol. 13, pp. 63–67.

———. 'Libraries in Iraq and Egypt: A Comparative Study', *International Library Review*, **9** 113–23 (January 1977).

Klibi, Chedly. 'ALDOC: Arab League Documentation Centre', Paper presented at the meeting of Arab information network, 2–4 November 1983, Baghdad.

Kostrewski, B.J., and Oppenheim, C. 'Ethics in Information Science', *Journal of Information Science*, **1**(5) 277–84 (1980).

Krek, Miroslav. 'Islamic Libraries', in *ALA World Encyclopedia of Library and Information Services*, R. Wedgeworth, (ed).Chicago, ALA, 1980.

Kurasman, Kathleen. 'Academic Library in Turkey', *International Library Review*, **12** 173–20 (April 1980).

Lamberton, D.M. (ed.). *Economics of Information and Knowledge*, Penguin, London, 1971.

Landheer, B. *Social Function of Libraries*, Scarecrow Press, New York, 1957.

Lawnga, T.K. 'Trends of Library Development in Uganda since 1962' in *International Librarianship*, Chandler, George, (ed.) London, Library Association, 1972.

Lerner, Daniel. *The Passing of Traditional Society*, New York, 1958.

Lim, Huch Tes. 'Libraries and Librarianship in Malaysia: 1817–1961', *Library History Review*, **2** 43–81 (May 1975).

———. *Libraries in West Malaysia and Singapore: A Short History*, Kuala Lumpur, University of Malaysia Library, 1970.

Lings, Martin. *Qur'anic Art of Calligraphy and Illumination*, World of Islam Festival Trust, London, 1976.

Lohrer, Allice. 'School Libraries in Iran and Near East', *ALA Bulletin*, **63** 1284–9 (July 1970).

Luckham, Bryan. *The Library in Society*, The Library Association, London, 1971.

Lyotard, Jean-Francois, *The Post-Modern Condition: A Report on Knowledge*, Manchester University Press, 1986.

Mackensen, Ruth S. 'Arabic Books and Libraries in the Umaiyad Period', *American Journal of Semitic Languages and Literature*, **51** 83–113 (1934–35);

51 114–25 (1934–35); **52** 22–33 (1935–36); **52** 104–10 (1935–36); **52** 245–53 (1935–36); **53** 239–50 (1936–37); **54** 41–61 (1937).

Madec, A. 'The Political Economy of Information Flows', *Intermedia*, **9**(2) 29–32 (1981).

Madkour, M.A.K. 'Information Processing and Retrieval in Arab Countries: Traditional Approaches and Modern Potentials', *UJISLAA*, **2**(2) 97–104 (1980).

Mahallati, Mozaffar-Eddin. *A Comparative Study of the Administration of the College Libraries at Isphahan, Jundi Shapur, and Pahlavi Universities*, MLS thesis, Shiraz, Pahlavi University, School of Graduate Studies, 1976.

Mahmood El-Hush, Abu Bakr. 'ALESCO and Special Library Collection in the Arab Countries', *UNESCO Journal of Information Science, Librarianship and Archives Administration*, **3** 57–9 (January–March 1981).

Makdisi, George. *The Rise of Colleges: Institutions of Learning in Islam and the West*, Edinburgh University Press, 1981.

Makdour, M.A.K. 'Information Processing and Retrieval in Arab Countries: Traditional Approaches and Modern Potentials', *UNESCO Journal of Information Science, Librarianship and Archives Administration*, **3** 97–104 (April–June 1980).

Mamoun, Izzel Din. 'Past, Present and Possible Future Developments of Librarianship in the Sudan', in *International Librarianship*, Chandler, George (ed.) London, Library Association, 1972.

Mangla, P.B. 'Libraries in Higher Education in Iran', *International Library Review*, **8** 173–200 (April 1976).

Manzoor, S. Parvez. 'The Thinking Artifice: AI and its Discontents', *Inquiry*, **3**(9) 34–9 (1986).

——. 'The Limits of Information', *Inquiry*, **4**(5) 44–8 (1987).

Masuda, Yoneji. 'Automatic State vs. Computopia: Unavoidable Alternatives for the Information Era', in *The Next 25 Years: Crisis and Opportunity*, Andrew A. Spekke (ed.) World Future Society, Washington D.C., 1975. See also his *The Information Society as Post-Industrial Society*, World Future Society, Washington D.C., 1980.

Matrai, L. 'Tradition and Innovation: Reading in a Changing Society', in *Reading in a Changing World*, F.E. Mohrhordt (ed.), Verlag Dokumentation, Munich, 1976.

Mattelart, A. 'Infotech and the Third World', *Radical Science*, **16** 27–35 (1985).

Mehdizadah, M.M. 'Libraries in Shiraz, Iran', *International Library Review*, **10** 327–32 (July 1978).

——. 'School Libraries in Fars Province, Iran', *International Library Review*, **10** 77–91 (January 1978).

Meherik, Mabrooka *et al.*, 'Libraries and Library Services in the Socialist Peoples Libyan Arab Jamahiriya', *International Library Review*, **13** 73–85 (January 1981).

Mehramy, Muhammad Aliasgharzadeh. *Adult Public and Children's Libraries in Eastern Azarbaijan Province*, MLS thesis, Shiraz, Pahlavi University, School of Graduate Studies, 1977.

Mohajir, A.R. 'Development of a National Scientific Information System with Reference to Pakistan', *Pakistan Library Bulletin*, **9** 29–46 (January–April 1977).

——. 'Information Needs of Science and Technology', *Pakistan Library Bulletin*, **8** 1–11 (Jan.–April 1977).

——. 'Meeting Information Needs for Socio-Economic Development', paper presented at the second COMLIS conference, Malaysia, 20–22 October 1986.

Mohammed, Oli. 'Islam, Knowledge and Librarianship', in *Library Education Across the Boundaries* . . . Anis Khurshid (ed.), University of Karachi, Karachi, 1981.

Mohammedally, Rafia. 'Information Training in Pakistan', *Information Development*, **1** 31–7 (1985).

Moran, M.L. 'Further Considerations on Romanization: Saudi Arabia', *International Library Review*, **13** 275–85 (July 1981).

Mun, Khoo Siew. 'University Libraries in Malaysia', in *International Handbook of Contemporary Developments in Librarianship*, Miles M. Jackson, (ed.) Westport, Connecticutt, Greenwood Press, 1981.

Mustafa, Muhammad Hassan. 'Library Service in the UNRAW Schools in Jordan', (In Arabic) *Risalat-al-Maktaba*, **15** (December 1980).

Mustafa, S.H. 'Amman Polytechnic Library', *Risalat-al-Maktaba*, **12** (June 1977).

Muydin, Abdul Aziz bin Shaik. 'Professionalization and Career Development Opportunities of Librarians in Malaysia', in *Education and Training for Librarianship in South-East Asia: Papers and Proceedings of Asian Librarians Held at the University of the Philippines, Quezon City December 10–14, 1973*, M.G. Dayit, *et al.* (ed.), Quezon City, University of the Philippines Library, 1973.

Al-Nadim, *The Fihrist of al-Nadim*, translated by Bayard Dodge, Columbia University Press, New York, 1970 (2 vols).

Al-Nahari, Abdul Aziz Muhammad. *The Role of National Libraries in Developing Countries with Special Reference to Saudi Arabia*, London, Mansell, 1984.

Nasim, Fatima. *Secondary School Library Resources in Karachi*, Karachi Library Promotion Bureau, 1984.

Nasution, A.S. 'Country Report on Library Development in Indonesia', in *Proceedings of the Third Conference of South East Asian Librarians, Jakarta, Indonesia, December 1–5, 1975*, Jakarta, 1977.

Natadjumena, Rachmat. 'An Indonesian National Library', *Australian Academic Research Libraries*, **8** 127–30 (September 1977).

El-Nouri, Anwar. 'Bibliographical Services in Kuwait in 1971', *Bibliography, Documentation, Terminology*, **13** 81–3 (March 1973).

Oakley, P. and Marsden David. *Approaches to Participation in Rural Development*, International Labour Office, Geneva, 1984.

Ogunsheye, F.A. 'Reading for Development in Urban Africa: The Case of Ibadan', in F.E. Mohrhordt, *op. cit.*

Oi Committee International (Compilers), *International development and the Human Environment: A Bibliography*, Collier Macmillan, London, 1974.

Omar, Ahmed Anwar. *al-Maktaba al-Far'iyya*, Cairo, 1971.

Osiobe, Stephen A. 'A Study of the Use of Information Sources by Medical Faculty Staff in Nigerian Universities', *Journal of Information Science*, **12** 177–83 (1986).

Paker, J.S. 'Library Development in the Sudan', *UNESCO Bulletin for Libraries*, **27** 78–83 (March–April 1973).

Pakistan Library Association, *Pakistan Librarianship*, 1970–71 and 1972–73; ed.

by Anis Khurshid (Karachi, 1972–73). 1974–75; ed. Mumtaz A. Anwar (Lahore, 1978).

Pantelidis, Veronica S. *The Arab World – Libraries and Librarianship 1960–1976: A Bibliography*, London, Mansell, 1979.

Pearson, J.D. 'Towards Total Bibliographic Control of Islamic Studies', *British Society for Middle Eastern Studies Bulletin*, **2**(2) 112–16 (1975).

Pearson, Lester. *Partners in Development*, Praeger, New York, 1969.

Pederson, J. *The Arabic Book*, translated by Geoffrey French, Princeton University Press, Princeton, New Jersey, 1984.

Porat, M.U. *The Information Economy*, vols. 1–9, Office of Telecommunication, US Department of Commerce, 1977.

Pourhamzel, Afsaueh. *Current Status of Library Education in Iran: A Review of Programmes Offered in Iranian Academic Institutions*, MLS thesis, Shiraz, Pahlavi University 1977.

Prakose, Mastini Harajo. 'Indonesia: Co-operative Programmes in Information', *International Library Review*, **8** 299–304 (October 1980).

——. 'Planning Interlending Systems for Developing Countries: A View from Indonesia', *Interlending Review*, **8** 114–16 (October 1980).

Pugwash Conference on Science and World Affairs, *Pugwash Guidelines for International Scientific Cooperation for Development*, London and Geneva, 1979.

Pui-Huen, P. Lim *et al*. *'Proceedings of the First Conference of the Southeast Asian Libraries*, Singapore, 1972.

Qazanchi, Fouad Y.M. 'Academic Libraries in Iraq', *Unesco Bulletin for Libraries*, **25** 91–3 (March–April 1971).

Qureshi, Naimuddin. 'The Development of Library and Information Services in Pakistan', in *Bowker Annual of Library and Book Trade Information 1978*, New York, Bowker.

——. 'The Education and Training of Librarians and Information Scientists in Pakistan', *Libri*, **29** 79–89 (March 1979).

Rashdi, Noor Ida Yang. 'Databases and Networks: Present Status and Prospects in the Muslim World', Paper presented at the Congress of Muslim Librarians and Information Scientists, 20–22 October 1986, Kedah, Malaysia.

Rayetz, Jerome. 'Computers and Ignorance', *Inquiry*, **3**(9) 40–44 (1986).

——. *Scientific Knowledge and Its Social Problems*, Oxford University Press, 1972.

'Regional Conference on the Development of Public Libraries in Africa'. *UNESCO Bulletin for Libraries*, **27**(2): March–April, 1963.

Rogers, Q. 'Towards a National Information Policy', *Bulletin of American Society of Information Science*, **2**(6) 13–15 (1976).

Rompas, John P. *Organisation and Development of Library and Information Service in a Developing Country: The Indonesian Case*, M.A. thesis, Loughborough, Loughborough University of Technology, 1978.

Rosenthal, F. *Knowledge Triumphant*, Brill, Leiden, 1970.

——. *Technique and Approach of Muslim Scholarship*, Pontificium Institutum Biblicum, Rome, 1947.

Rostow, W.W. *Stages of Economic Growth*, Cambridge University Press, 1963.

Rumi, Jalaluddin, *Teachings of Rumi: The Masnavi*, abridged and translated by E.H. Whinfield, The Octagon Press, London, 1973.

Sabzwari, Ghaniul Akram. 'Universal Islamic Classification', *Pakistan Library Bulletin*, **13**(2) 1–20 (1982).

Said, Omar H. 'Status of Special Libraries in Jordan', *Risalat- al-Maktaba*, **14** (December/January 1978/79).

Sajjad ur Rahman 'Databases and Networks: Present Status and Prospects in the Muslim World', paper presented at the second COMLIS meeting, Malaysia, 20–22 October 1986.

Salem, S. 'The Role of Information in Science and Technology Transfer in Arab Countries', *Journal of Information Science*, **2** 255–61 (November 1980).

——. 'Information Infrastructure in the Arab Countries: An Analysis', *Journal of Information Science*, **12** 217–230 (1986).

Samimi, Mehrangeez. *Library Use and Academic Research in Iran in the Sciences, Social Sciences and Humanities*, MLS thesis, Shiraz, Pahlavi University, School of Graduate Studies, 1976.

Sardar, Ziauddin. 'Between GIN and TWIN: Meeting the Information Needs of the Third World', *Aslib Proceedings*, **33**(2) 53–61 (1981).

——. 'Civilizational Dialogue, Captured Minds and the Technology of the Intellect', *Muslim World Book Review*, **7**(1) 3–10 (1986).

——. 'Contemporary Librarianship and Information Science in the Muslim World: A Select Bibliography 1970–1987', *Muslim World Book Review*, **7**(3) 58–65 (1987).

——. 'The Hajj — A Select Bibliography', *Muslim World Book Review*, **3**(1) 57–66 (1982).

——. 'The Information Unit of the Hajj Research Centre', *Aslib Proceedings*, **30** 158–64 (May 1978).

——. 'Intellectual Space and Western Domination: Abstracts, Bibliographies and Current Awareness', *Muslim World Book Review*, **4**(2) 3–8 (1984).

——. 'Last Chance for World Unity', *New Scientist* **91** 334–41 (1981).

——. 'Middle East', in *Science and Government Report International Almanac 1978–1979*, Daniel S. Greenberg and Anne D. Norman (eds.), Washington, D.C., Science and Government Report (1979).

——. 'Redirecting Science towards Islam: An Examination of Islamic and Western Approaches to Knowledge and Values', *Hamdard Islamicus*, **9**(1) 23–34 (1986).

——. 'Saudi Arabia: Indigenous Sources of Information', *Aslib Proceedings*, **31** 237–44 (May 1979).

——. 'Saudi Arabia Places U.S. Databases On-line', *Middle East Computing*, No. 3, 9–10 (September 1982).

——. 'Science and Technology in the Muslim World — A Select Bibliography', *Muslim World Book Review*, **4**(3) 58–65 (1984).

——. 'Scientific Thinking behind Khomeini', *Nature*, **282** 439–41 (1979).

——. 'Systems to Play Key Role in Saudi Growth', *Middle East Computing*, No. 4, 12–13 (November 1982).

——. 'What does the Third World really want? Expectations and Reality in the North-South Dialogue at UNCSATD' in *World Interdependence and Economic Co-operation among Developing Countries*, Centre for Applied Studies in International Negotiations, Geneva (1982).

——. and Rosser-Owen, Dawud G. 'Science Policy and Developing Countries', in *Science, Technology and Society: A Cross-disciplinary Perspective*, Ina Spiegel-Rosing and Derek de Solla Price (eds.), Sage, London, 1977.

Sarwar, Hussain. 'Library Associations in Bangladesh', *International Library Review* , **13** 323–7 (July 1981).

——. 'Library Education in Bangladesh: Yesterday and Today', *UNESCO Journal of Information Science, Librarianship and Archives Administration,* **2** 180–83 (July–September 1980).

Sasono, Adi and Akhmadi, Heri. 'Islamic Studies Information Exchange: A Proposal for Islamic Library Networking', Paper presented at the Congress of Muslim Librarians and Information Scientists, 20–22 October 1986, Kedah, Malaysia.

Sattar, A. 'Scope for Information Exchange: Programmes among Muslim Countries Science and Technology', Paper presented at the Congress of Muslim Librarians and Information Scientists, 20–22 October 1986, Kedah, Malaysia.

Sattar, A., and Sajjad ur Rehman. 'Coverage of Islamic Literature in Selected Indexing Services', *International Library Review,* **17**(4) 357–70 (1985).

Schwoeroel, H. 'Industrial Information: A Guide to better understanding and indications of how to use assistance and services offered by UNIDO in introducing information as an instrument for industrialization', in *Information System Design and Socio-Economic Development,* FID, The Hague, 1976.

Senassa, Abdolhassan. *History of Academic, Religious, Private and Public Libraries in Shiraz from the Constitutional Revolution to the Shah-and-People Revolution,* MLS thesis, Shiraz, Pahlavi University, School of Graduate Studies, 1977.

Seymour, Ian, *OPEC: Instrument of Change,* Macmillan, London, 1980.

Sezgin, Faut. *Geschichte des Arabischen Schrifttums,* Brill, Leiden, 1974–82 (8 Volumes published).

Shahar, Banun Jaafar. 'Computerized Library and Information Networking: A Malaysian Perspective', Paper presented at the Singapore/Malaysia Congress of Librarians and Information Scientists, 4–6 September 1986, Singapore.

Shahnaz, Khadivi. *A Survey of the Public Libraries for Adults and Children in the Province of Isfahan,* MLS thesis, Shiraz, Pahlavi University, School of Graduate Studies, 1977.

Shamsul Alam, A.K.M. 'Libraries and Library Problems of Bangladesh', *UNESCO Bulletin for Libraries,* **27** 262–64 (September–October 1973).

Sharif, A. 'The Factors Which Affect the Development of Librarianship and Library Education in Arab Countries', *International Library Review,* **11** 245–57 (1979).

——. 'The Development of Professional Library Education in the Arab Countries', *International Library Review,* **13** 87–101 (January 1981).

Shehadeh, Lilly. 'Biblioteker-i-Qatar', *Bibliotek,* **70**(10) 311–14 (1980).

Shera, J.H. *The Sociological Foundation of Librarianship,* Asia, Bombay, 1970.

Sibai, Mohamed Makki. *Mosque Libraries in Islamic Life and Culture,* London, Mansell, 1987.

Siddique, A.B. 'Subscribing to Foreign Periodicals in Bangladesh', *Herald of Library Science,* **17** 275–80 (October 1978).

Siddiqui, Akhtar H. *Library Development in Pakistan,* Lahore, Student Services, 1976.

Siddiqui, Muhammad Nejatullah. *Muslim Economic Thinking: A Survey of Contemporary Literature,* Leicester, The Islamic Foundation, 1981.

Simsova, S. *et al.*, *A Handbook of Comparative Librarianship*, 2nd edn. Hamden Conn. Clive Bingley, 1975.

Sinai, A. 'The Impact of Recent Development on Iranian Librarianship', in *International Librarianship*, Chandler, George (ed.), London, The Library Association, 1972.

———. 'Iranian Documentation Centre (IRANDOC)', In *Encyclopedia of Library and Information Science*, New York, Marcel Dekker, 1975.

Sklair, Leslie. *Organised Knowledge*, Paladin, 1973.

Sluglett, Peter. *Theses on Islam, the Middle East and North-West Africa, 1880-1978*, London, Mansell, 1983.

Society for the Promotion and Improvement of Libraries, *Role of the Library in National Reconstruction*, Hamdard National Foundation, Karachi, 1971.

Spero, J. 'Information and Telecommunications is a Trade Issue', *Intermedia*, **10**(2) 9–11 (1982).

Suhail, Manzoor. 'Trends of Library Users: A Study of Iraqi Scene', *Ind. Lib.* **35** 9–17 (June 1980).

———. 'Saudi Arabian National Centre for Science and Technology (SANCST) database', *International Library Review* **17**(1985) pp. 77–90.

Talukdar, Alauddin. 'Bangladesh Institute of Development Studies and its Socio-Economic Information Services', *UNESCO Bulletin for Libraries*, **32** 178–83 (May–June 1978).

Tamby, Zaleha. 'Research Resources for the Study of Islam in Southeast Asia', paper presented at the Congress of Muslim Librarians and Information Scientists, 20–22 October 1986, Kedah, Malaysia.

Tell, B.V. 'The awakening information needs of the developing countries', *Journal of Information Science*, **1**(5) 285–90 (1980).

Thorpe, P. 'The Impact of New Information Technology in the Developing Countries', *Journal of Information Science*, **8**(5) 213–20, 1984.

Umapathy, K.S. 'Libraries and Librarianship in Iran', *International Library Review*, **10** 119–35 (April 1970).

Umaruddin, Muhammad. *The Ethical Philosophy of al-Ghazzali*, Ashraf, Lahore, 1962.

Usmani, M. Adil. *Bibliographic Services Throughout Pakistan*, Karachi, Dr. Mahmud Husain Library, University of Karachi, 1978.

———. *Islamic Studies: Literature on Quran in English*, Karachi, Islamic Documentation and Information Centre, 1984.

——— and Siddiqui, Akhtar H. *A Bibliography of Doctoral Dissertations on Islam*, Karachi, Islamic Documentation and Information Centre, 1985.

Weinir, M. *Modernisation: The Dynamic of Growth*, Basic Books, New York, 1966.

Wesley, Cecile. 'Information on Current Research in Sudan', *Information Development*, **1** 217–22 (October 1985).

WHO, *Report on a WHO/UNICEF Intersectoral Workshop on Primary Health Care*, Geneva, 1982, annex.

Wiener, Norbert. *The Human Use of Human Beings: Cybernetics and society*, MIT Press, Cambridge, Massachusetts, 1948.

———. *Cybernetics or Control and Communication in Animals and Machines*, MIT Press, Cambridge, Massachusetts, 1948.

Wijasuriya, D.E.K. 'Policies and Libraries: The Malaysian Experience', in

Education and Training for Librarianship in South-East Asia: Papers and Pro-ceedings of the Second Conference of South-East Asian Librarians held at the University of the Philippines, Quezon City, December 10-14 1973, ed. M.G. Dayrit, *et al.* Quezon City, University of the Philippines Library 1975.

——. 'Library and Information Science Education and Training in Malaysia', *Library News* (Ceylon National Library Service Board) **5** 6-9 (Jan.-March 1977).

——. 'Malaysia: The Development of Library Services', *Information Develop-ment,* **1** 74-84 (April 1985).

——. 'The Development of National Information Systems', *Journal of Informa-tion Science,* **1**(1) 27-34 (1979).

—— *et al. The Barefoot Librarian, Library Development in Southeast Asia with Special Reference to Malaysia,* London, Clive Bingley, 1975.

Woodward, A.M. 'Future information requirements of the third world', *Journal of Information Science,* **1**(5) 259-66 (1980).

Yaghmai, N.; Shahla, Diodato; Virgil, P., and Maxin, J.A. 'Arab-Islamic Cultures and on-Line Bibliographical Systems', *International Library Review,* **18**(1) 15-24 (1986).

Yovits, M.C., Rose L. and Abilock J. 'Development of a theory of information flow and analysis', in *Many Faces of Information Science,* E.C. Weiss (ed.), Westview Press, Colorado, 1977.

Zafar, Syed Ahmad. *University Libraries in Muslim Countries: Basic Statistics,* Jeddah, Deanship of Library Affairs, King Abdul Aziz University, 1986.

Zahawi, Faria. 'The Development of the Arab League Documentation Centre (ALDOC) and Plans of the Arab Information System Network (ARISNET)', Paper presented at the Congress of Muslim Librarians and Information Scientists, 20-22 October 1986, Kedah, Malaysia.

Zehery, Mohammad H. 'Libraries and Librarianship in Kuwait', *International Library Review,* **7** 3-13 (January 1975).

——. *Library Service in Kuwait: A Survey and Analysis with Recommendations for Public Library Development,*Ph.D. dissertation, Ann Arbor, Michigan: Uni-versity Microfilms, 1975.

——. 'Special Libraries in Kuwait', *Special Libraries,* **66** 595-602 (December 1975).

Index

Scope: the index includes references to persons, organizations, publications, and subjects; authors cited in the text have been indexed, but not footnotes and bibliographical references. Arrangement: alphabetization is word by word; in Arabic names the prefix "al-" is ignored for filing.